WITHOUT FEATHERS

Without Feathers

. . . .

Woody Allen

 Random House • N E W Y O R K

All rights reserved under International and Pan-American Copyright Conventions. Published in the United States by Random House, Inc., New York, and simultaneously in Canada by Random House of Canada Limited, Toronto.

"No Kaddish for Weinstein," "Fine Times: An Oral Memoir," "Examining Psychic Phenomena," "A Guide to Some of the Lesser Ballets," "The Early Essays," "Selections from the Allen Notebooks," "Lovborg's Women Considered," and "The Whore of Mensa" appeared originally in *The New Yorker.* "Fabulous Tales and Mythical Beasts," "The Irish Genius," and "The Scrolls" first appeared in *The New Republic.* "Match Wits with Inspector Ford" originally appeared in *Playboy* Magazine. "A Brief, Yet Helpful, Guide to Civil Disobedience" appeared in *The New York Times,* July 15, 1972. Reprinted by permission.

Library of Congress Cataloging in Publication Data
Allen, Woody.
Without feathers.
I. Title.
PS3551.L44W5   818'.5'407   74-29597
ISBN 0-394-49743-0

Manufactured in the United States of America
987

"Hope is the thing with feathers . . ."
—Emily Dickinson

CONTENTS

WITHOUT FEATHERS

Selections from the Allen Notebooks

Following are excerpts from the hitherto secret private journal of Woody Allen, which will be published posthumously or after his death, whichever comes first.

Getting through the night is becoming harder and harder. Last evening, I had the uneasy feeling that some men were trying to break into my room to shampoo me. But why? I kept imagining I saw shadowy forms, and at 3 A.M. the underwear I had draped over a chair resembled the Kaiser on roller skates. When I finally did fall asleep, I had that same hideous nightmare in which a woodchuck is trying to claim my prize at a raffle. Despair.

I believe my consumption has grown worse. Also my asthma. The wheezing comes and goes, and I get dizzy more and more frequently. I have taken to violent choking and fainting. My room is damp and I have perpetual chills and palpitations of the heart. I noticed, too, that I am out of napkins. Will it never stop?

Idea for a story: A man awakens to find his parrot has been made Secretary of Agriculture. He is consumed with jealousy and shoots himself, but unfortunately the gun is the type with a little flag that pops out, with the word "Bang" on it. The flag pokes his eye out, and he lives—a chastened human being who, for the first time, enjoys the simple pleasures of life, like farming or sitting on an air hose.

Thought: Why does man kill? He kills for food. And not only food: frequently there must be a beverage.

Should I marry W.? Not if she won't tell me the other letters in her name. And what about her career? How can I ask a woman of her beauty to give up the Roller Derby? Decisions . . .

Once again I tried committing suicide—this time by wetting my nose and inserting it into the light socket. Unfortunately, there was a short in the wiring, and I merely caromed off the icebox. Still obsessed by thoughts of death, I brood constantly. I keep wondering if there is an afterlife, and if there is will they be able to break a twenty?

I ran into my brother today at a funeral. We had not seen one another for fifteen years, but as usual he produced a pig bladder from his pocket and began hitting me on the head with it. Time has helped me understand him better. I finally realize his remark that I am "some loathsome vermin fit only for extermination" was said more out of compassion than anger. Let's face it: he was always much brighter than me—wittier, more cultured, better educated. Why he is still working at McDonald's is a mystery.

Idea for story: Some beavers take over Carnegie Hall and perform *Wozzeck*. (Strong theme. What will be the structure?)

Good Lord, why am I so guilty? Is it because I hated my father? Probably it was the veal-parmigian' incident. Well, what *was* it doing in his wallet? If I had listened to him, I would be blocking hats for a living. I can hear him now:

"To block hats—that is everything." I remember his reaction when I told him I wanted to write. "The only writing you'll do is in collaboration with an owl." I still have no idea what he meant. What a sad man! When my first play, *A Cyst for Gus*, was produced at the Lyceum, he attended opening night in tails and a gas mask.

Today I saw a red-and-yellow sunset and thought, How insignificant I am! Of course, I thought that yesterday, too, and it rained. I was overcome with self-loathing and contemplated suicide again—this time by inhaling next to an insurance salesman.

Short story: A man awakens in the morning and finds himself transformed into his own arch supports. (This idea can work on many levels. Psychologically, it is the quintessence of Kruger, Freud's disciple who discovered sexuality in bacon.)

How wrong Emily Dickinson was! Hope is not "the thing with feathers." The thing with feathers has turned out to be my nephew. I must take him to a specialist in Zurich.

I have decided to break off my engagement with W. She doesn't understand my writing, and said last night that my *Critique of Metaphysical Reality* reminded her of *Airport*. We quarreled, and she brought up the subject of children again, but I convinced her they would be too young.

Do I believe in God? I did until Mother's accident. She fell on some meat loaf, and it penetrated her spleen. She lay in a coma for months, unable to do anything but sing "Granada" to an imaginary herring. Why was this woman in the prime of life so afflicted—because in her youth she dared to defy convention and got married with a brown paper bag on her head? And how can I believe in God when just last week I got my tongue caught in the roller of an electric typewriter? I am plagued by doubts. What if everything is an illusion and nothing exists? In that case, I definitely overpaid for my carpet. If only God would give me some clear sign! Like making a large deposit in my name at a Swiss bank.

Had coffee with Melnick today. He talked to me about his idea of having all government officials dress like hens.

Play idea: A character based on my father, but without quite so prominent a big toe. He is sent to the Sorbonne to study the harmonica. In the end, he dies, never realizing his one dream—to sit up to his waist in gravy. (I see a brilliant second-act curtain, where two midgets come upon a severed head in a shipment of volleyballs.)

While taking my noon walk today, I had more morbid thoughts. What *is* it about death that bothers me so much? Probably the hours. Melnick says the soul is immortal and lives on after the body drops away, but if my soul exists without my body I am convinced all my clothes will be too loose-fitting. Oh, well . . .

Did not have to break off with W. after all, for as luck would have it, she ran off to Finland with a professional circus geek. All for the best, I suppose, although I had another of those attacks where I start coughing out of my ears.

Last night, I burned all my plays and poetry. Ironically, as I was burning my masterpiece, *Dark Penguin*, the room caught fire, and I am now the object of a lawsuit by some men named Pinchunk and Schlosser. Kierkegaard was right.

Examining Psychic Phenomena

There is no question that there is an unseen world. The problem is, how far is it from midtown and how late is it open? Unexplainable events occur constantly. One man will see spirits. Another will hear voices. A third will wake up and find himself running in the Preakness. How many of us have not at one time or another felt an ice-cold hand on the back of our neck while we were home alone? (Not me, thank God, but some have.) What is behind these experiences? Or in front of them, for that matter? Is it true that some men can foresee the future or communicate with ghosts? And after death is it still possible to take showers?

Fortunately, these questions about psychic phenomena are answered in a soon to be published book, *Boo!*, by Dr. Osgood Mulford Twelge, the noted parapsychologist and professor of ectoplasm at Columbia University. Dr. Twelge has assembled a remarkable history of supernatural incidents that covers the whole range of psychic phenomena, from thought transference to the bizarre experience of two brothers on opposite parts of the globe, one of whom took a bath while the other suddenly got clean. What follows is but a sampling of Dr. Twelge's most celebrated cases, with his comments.

APPARITIONS
· · · · · · · ·

On March 16, 1882, Mr. J. C. Dubbs awoke in the middle of the night and saw his brother Amos, who had been dead for fourteen years, sitting at the foot of his bed flicking chickens. Dubbs asked his brother what he was doing there, and his brother said not to worry, he was dead and was only in town for the weekend. Dubbs asked his brother what it was like in "the other world," and his brother said it was not unlike Cleveland. He said he had returned to give Dubbs a message, which was that a dark-blue suit and Argyle socks are a big mistake.

At that point, Dubbs's servant girl entered and saw Dubbs talking to "a shapeless, milky haze," which she said reminded her of Amos Dubbs but was a little better-looking. Finally, the ghost asked Dubbs to join him in an aria from *Faust*, which the two sang with great fervor. As dawn rose, the ghost walked through the wall, and Dubbs, trying to follow, broke his nose.

This appears to be a classic case of the apparition phenomenon, and if Dubbs is to be believed, the ghost returned again and caused Mrs. Dubbs to rise out of a chair and hover over the dinner table for twenty minutes until she dropped into some gravy. It is interesting to note that spirits have a tendency to be mischievous, which A. F. Childe, the British mystic, attributes to a marked feeling of inferiority they have over being dead. "Apparitions" are often associated with individuals who have suffered an unusual demise. Amos Dubbs, for instance, had died under mysterious circumstances when a farmer accidentally planted him along with some turnips.

Spirit Departure
. . . .

Mr. Albert Sykes reports the following experience: "I was sitting having biscuits with some friends when I felt my spirit leave my body and go make a telephone call. For some reason, it called the Moscowitz Fiber Glass Company. My spirit then returned to my body and sat for another twenty minutes or so, hoping nobody would suggest charades. When the conversation turned to mutual funds, it left again and began wandering around the city. I am convinced that it visited the Statue of Liberty and then saw the stage show at Radio City Music Hall. Following that, it went to Benny's Steak House and ran up a tab of sixty-eight dollars. My spirit then decided to return to my body, but it was impossible to get a cab. Finally, it walked up Fifth Avenue and rejoined me just in time to catch the late news. I could tell that it was reentering my body, because I felt a sudden chill, and a voice said, 'I'm back. You want to pass me those raisins?'

"This phenomenon has happened to me several times since. Once, my spirit went to Miami for a weekend, and once it was arrested for trying to leave Macy's without paying for a tie. The fourth time, it was actually my body that left my spirit, although all it did was get a rubdown and come right back."

Spirit departure was very common around 1910, when many "spirits" were reported wandering aimlessly around India searching for the American Consulate. The phenomenon is quite similar to transubstantiation, the process whereby a person will suddenly dematerialize and rematerialize somewhere else in the world. This is not a bad way to travel, although there is usually a half-hour wait for luggage. The most astonishing case of transubstantiation was that of Sir Arthur Nurney, who vanished with an audible *pop* while he was taking a bath and suddenly appeared in the string section of the Vienna Symphony Orchestra. He stayed on as the first violinist for twenty-seven years, although he could only play "Three Blind Mice," and vanished abruptly one day during Mozart's Jupiter Symphony, turning up in bed with Winston Churchill.

PRECOGNITION
. . . .

Mr. Fenton Allentuck describes the following precognitive dream: "I went to sleep at midnight and dreamed that I was playing whist with a plate of chives. Suddenly the dream shifted, and I saw my grandfather about to be run over by a truck in the middle of the street, where he was waltzing with a clothing dummy. I tried to scream, but when I opened my mouth the only sound that came out was chimes, and my grandfather was run over.

"I awoke in a sweat and ran to my grandfather's house and asked him if he had plans to go waltzing with a clothing dummy. He said of course not, although he had contemplated posing as a shepherd to fool his enemies. Relieved, I walked home, but learned later that the old man had slipped on a chicken-salad sandwich and fallen off the Chrysler Building."

Precognitive dreams are too common to be dismissed as pure coincidence. Here a man dreams of a relative's death, and it occurs. Not everyone is so lucky. J. Martinez, of Kennebunkport, Maine, dreamed he won the Irish Sweepstakes. When he awoke, his bed had floated out to sea.

TRANCES
. . . . . .

Sir Hugh Swiggles, the skeptic, reports an interesting séance experience:

> We attended the home of Madame Reynaud, the noted medium, where we were all told to sit around the table and join hands. Mr. Weeks couldn't stop giggling, and Madame Reynaud smashed him on the head with a Ouija board. The lights were turned out, and Madame Reynaud attempted to contact Mrs. Marple's husband, who had died at the opera when his beard caught fire. The following is an exact transcript:
>
> MRS. MARPLE: What do you see?
>
> MEDIUM: I see a man with blue eyes and a pinwheel hat.
>
> MRS. MARPLE: That's my husband!
>
> MEDIUM: His name is . . . Robert. No . . . Richard . . .
>
> MRS. MARPLE: Quincy.
>
> MEDIUM: Quincy! Yes, that's it!
>
> MRS. MARPLE: What else about him?
>
> MEDIUM: He is bald but usually keeps some leaves on his head so nobody will notice.
>
> MRS. MARPLE: Yes! Exactly!
>
> MEDIUM: For some reason, he has an object . . . a loin of pork.
>
> MRS. MARPLE: My anniversary present to him! Can you make him speak?
>
> MEDIUM: Speak, spirit. Speak.
>
> QUINCY: Claire, this is Quincy.
>
> MRS. MARPLE: Oh, Quincy! Quincy!
>
> QUINCY: How long do you keep the chicken in when you're trying to broil it?
>
> MRS. MARPLE: That voice! It's him!
>
> MEDIUM: Everybody concentrate.

MRS. MARPLE: Quincy, are they treating you okay?

QUINCY: Not bad, except it takes four days to get your cleaning back.

MRS. MARPLE: Quincy, do you miss me?

QUINCY: Huh? Oh, er, sure. Sure, kid. I got to be going. . . .

MEDIUM: I'm losing it. He's fading. . . .

I found this séance to pass the most stringent tests of credulity, with the minor exception of a phonograph, which was found under Madame Reynaud's dress.

There is no doubt that certain events recorded at séances are genuine. Who does not recall the famous incident at Sybil Seretsky's, when her goldfish sang "I Got Rhythm"— a favorite tune of her recently deceased nephew? But contacting the dead is at best difficult, since most deceased are reluctant to speak up, and those that do seem to hem and haw before getting to the point. The author has actually seen a table rise, and Dr. Joshua Fleagle, of Harvard, attended a séance in which a table not only rose but excused itself and went upstairs to sleep.

CLAIRVOYANCE
· · · · · · · · ·

One of the most astounding cases of clairvoyance is that of the noted Greek psychic, Achille Londos. Londos realized he had "unusual powers" by the age of ten, when he could lie in bed and, by concentrating, make his father's false teeth jump out of his mouth. After a neighbor's husband had been missing for three weeks, Londos told them to look in the stove, where the man was found knitting. Londos could concentrate on a person's face and force the image to come out on a roll of ordinary Kodak film, although he could never seem to get anybody to smile.

In 1964, he was called in to aid police in capturing the Düsseldorf Strangler, a fiend who always left a baked Alaska on the chests of his victims. Merely by sniffing a handkerchief, Londos led police to Siegfried Lenz, handyman at a school for deaf turkeys, who said he was the strangler and could he please have his handkerchief back.

Londos is just one of many people with psychic powers. C. N. Jerome, the psychic, of Newport, Rhode Island, claims he can guess any card being thought of by a squirrel.

PROGNOSTICATION

Finally, we come to Aristonidis, the sixteenth-century count whose predictions continue to dazzle and perplex even the most skeptical. Typical examples are:

"Two nations will go to war, but only one will win."

(Experts feel this probably refers to the Russo-Japanese War of 1904–05—an astounding feat of prognostication, considering the fact that it was made in 1540.)

"A man in Istanbul will have his hat blocked, and it will be ruined."

(In 1860, Abu Hamid, Ottoman warrior, sent his cap out to be cleaned, and it came back with spots.)

"I see a great person, who one day will invent for mankind a garment to be worn over his trousers for protection while cooking. It will be called an 'abron' or 'aprone.' "

(Aristonidis meant the apron, of course.)

"A leader will emerge in France. He will be very short and will cause great calamity."

(This is a reference either to Napoleon or to Marcel Lumet, an eighteenth-century midget who instigated a plot to rub béarnaise sauce on Voltaire.)

"In the New World, there will be a place named California, and a man named Joseph Cotten will become famous."

(No explanation necessary.)

A Guide to Some of the Lesser Ballets

DMITRI
· · · · · ·

The ballet opens at a carnival. There are refreshments and rides. Many people in gaily colored costumes dance and laugh, to the accompaniment of flutes and woodwinds, while the trombones play in a minor key to suggest that soon the refreshments will run out and everybody will be dead.

Wandering around the fairgrounds is a beautiful girl named Natasha, who is sad because her father has been sent to fight in Khartoum, and there is no war there. Following her is Leonid, a young student, who is too shy to speak to Natasha but places a mixed-green salad on her doorstep every night. Natasha is moved by the gift and wishes she could meet the man who is sending it, particularly since she hates the house dressing and would prefer Roquefort.

The two strangers accidentally meet when Leonid, trying to compose a love note to Natasha, falls out of the Ferris wheel. She helps him up, and the two dance a pas de deux, after which Leonid tries to impress her by rolling his eyes until he has to be carried to the comfort station. Leonid offers profuse apologies and suggests that the two of them stroll to Tent No. 5 and watch a puppet show—an invitation that confirms in Natasha's mind the idea that she is dealing with an idiot.

The puppet show, however, is enchanting, and a large, amusing puppet named Dmitri falls in love with Natasha. She realizes that although he is only sawdust, he has a soul, and when he suggests checking into a hotel as Mr. and Mrs. John Doe, she is excited. The two dance a pas de deux, despite the fact that she just danced a pas de deux and is perspiring like an ox. Natasha confesses her love for Dmitri and swears that the two of them will always be together, even though the man who works his strings will have to sleep on a cot in the parlor.

Leonid, outraged at being thrown over for a puppet, shoots Dmitri, who doesn't die but appears on the roof of the Merchants Bank, drinking haughtily from a bottle of Air Wick. The action becomes confused, and there is much rejoicing when Natasha fractures her skull.

THE SACRIFICE
. . . .

A melodic prelude recounts man's relation to the earth and why he always seems to wind up buried in it. The curtain rises on a vast primitive wasteland, not unlike certain parts of New Jersey. Men and women sit in separate groups and then begin to dance, but they have no idea why and soon sit down again. Presently a young male in the prime of life enters and dances a hymn to fire. Suddenly it is discovered he is *on* fire, and after being put out he slinks off. Now the stage becomes dark, and Man challenges Nature—a stirring encounter during which Nature is bitten on the hip, with the result that for the next six months the temperature never rises above thirteen degrees.

Scene 2 opens, and Spring still has not come, although it is late August and no one is quite sure when to set the clocks ahead. The elders of the tribe meet and decide to propitiate Nature by sacrificing a young girl. A maiden is selected. She is given three hours to report to the outskirts of town, where she is told they are having a weenie roast. When the girl appears that night, she asks where all the frankfurters are. She is ordered by the elders to dance herself to death. She pleads pathetically, telling them that she is not that good a dancer. The villagers insist, and, as the music builds relentlessly, the girl spins in a frenzy, achieving sufficient centrifugal force to hurl her silver fillings across a football field. Everyone rejoices, but too soon, for not only does Spring fail to come but two of the elders get subpoenaed in a mail-fraud charge.

THE SPELL
· · · · · · ·

The overture begins with the brass in a joyous mood, while underneath, the double basses seem to be warning us, "Don't listen to the brass. What the hell does brass know?" Presently, the curtain rises on Prince Sigmund's palace, magnificent in its splendor and rent-controlled. It is the Prince's twenty-first birthday, but he grows despondent as he opens his gifts because most of them turn out to be pajamas. One by one, his old friends pay their respects, and he greets them with a handshake or a slap on the back, depending on which way they are facing. He reminisces with his oldest friend, Wolfschmidt, and they vow that if either of them grows bald the other will wear a toupee. The ensemble dances in preparation for the hunt until Sigmund says, "What hunt?" No one is quite sure, but the revelry has gone too far, and when the check comes there is much anger.

Bored with life, Sigmund dances his way down to the

shore of the lake, where he stares at his perfect reflection for
forty minutes, annoyed at not having brought his shaving
equipment. Suddenly he hears the flutter of wings, and a
group of wild swans flies across the moon; they take the first
right and head back to the Prince. Sigmund is astounded to
see that their leader is part swan and part woman—unfortunately, divided lengthwise. She enchants Sigmund, who is
careful not to make any poultry jokes. The two dance a pas
de deux that ends when Sigmund throws his back out.
Yvette, the Swan Woman, tells Sigmund that she is under a
spell cast by a magician named Von Epps, and that because
of her appearance it is nearly impossible to get a bank loan.
In an especially difficult solo, she explains, in dance
language, that the only way to lift Von Epps's curse is for
her lover to go to secretarial school and learn shorthand.
This is odious to Sigmund, but he swears he will. Suddenly
Von Epps appears, in the form of yesterday's laundry, and
spirits Yvette away with him as the first act ends.

As Act II begins, it is a week later, and the Prince is
about to be married to Justine, a woman he had completely
forgotten about. Sigmund is torn by ambivalent feelings
because he still loves the Swan Woman, but Justine is very
beautiful, too, and has no major drawbacks like feathers or
a beak. Justine dances seductively around Sigmund, who
seems to be debating whether to go through with the
marriage or find Yvette and see if the doctors can come up
with anything. Cymbals crash and Von Epps, the Magician, enters. Actually, he was not invited to the wedding,
but he promises not to eat much. Furious, Sigmund pulls his
sword and stabs Von Epps through the heart. This casts a
pall on the party, and Sigmund's mother commands the
chef to wait a few minutes before bringing out the roast
beef.

Meanwhile, Wolfschmidt, acting on Sigmund's behalf,
has found the missing Yvette—not a difficult task, he
explains, "because how many half women, half swans are

there hanging around Hamburg?" Despite Justine's imploring, Sigmund rushes off to Yvette. Justine runs after him and kisses him, as the orchestra strikes a minor chord and we realize Sigmund has his leotards on inside out. Yvette weeps, explaining that the only way to lift the spell is for her to die. In one of the most moving and beautiful passages in any ballet, she runs headlong into a brick wall. Sigmund watches her body change from a dead swan to a dead woman and realizes how bittersweet life can be, particularly for fowl. Grief-stricken, he decides to join her, and after a delicate dance of mourning he swallows a barbell.

THE PREDATORS
. . . .

This celebrated electronic ballet is perhaps the most dramatic of all modern dances. It begins with an overture of contemporary sounds—street noises, ticking clocks, a dwarf playing "Hora Staccato" on a comb and tissue paper. The curtain then rises on a blank stage. For several minutes, nothing happens; eventually, the curtain falls and there is an intermission.

Act II begins with a hush as some young men dance on, pretending to be insects. The leader is a common housefly, while the others resemble a variety of garden pests. They move sinuously to the dissonant music, in search of an immense buttered roll, which gradually appears in the background. They are about to eat it when they are interrupted by a procession of women who carry a large can of Raid. Panic-stricken, the males try to escape, but they are put into metal cages, with nothing to read. The women dance orgiastically around the cages, preparing to devour the males the minute they can find some soy sauce. As the females prepare to dine, one young girl notices a forlorn male, with drooping antennae. She is drawn to him, and the two dance slowly to French horns as he whispers in her ear,

"Don't eat me." The two fall in love, and make elaborate plans for a nuptial flight, but the female changes her mind and devours the male, preferring instead to move in with a roommate.

A Day in the Life of a Doe

Unbearably lovely music is heard as the curtain rises, and we see the woods on a summer afternoon. A fawn dances on and nibbles slowly at some leaves. He drifts lazily through the soft foliage. Soon he starts coughing and drops dead.

The Scrolls

Scholars will recall that several years ago a shepherd, wandering in the Gulf of Aqaba, stumbled upon a cave containing several large clay jars and also two tickets to the ice show. Inside the jars were discovered six parchment scrolls with ancient incomprehensible writing which the shepherd, in his ignorance, sold to the museum for $750,000 apiece. Two years later the jars turned up in a pawnshop in Philadelphia. One year later the shepherd turned up in a pawnshop in Philadelphia and neither was claimed.

Archaeologists originally set the date of the scrolls at 4000 B.C., or just after the massacre of the Israelites by their benefactors. The writing is a mixture of Sumerian, Aramaic, and Babylonian and seems to have been done by either one man over a long period of time, or several men who shared the same suit. The authenticity of the scrolls is currently in great doubt, particularly since the word "Oldsmobile" appears several times in the text, and the few fragments that have finally been translated deal with familiar religious themes in a more than dubious way. Still, excavationist A. H. Bauer has noted that even though the fragments seem totally fraudulent, this is probably the greatest archeological find in history with the exception of the recovery of his cuff links from a tomb in Jerusalem. The following are the translated fragments.

One . . . And the Lord made an bet with Satan to test Job's loyalty and the Lord, for no apparent reason to Job, smote him on the head and again on the ear and pushed him into an thick sauce so as to make Job sticky and vile and then He slew a tenth part of Job's kine and Job calleth out: "Why doth thou slay my kine? Kine are hard to come by. Now I am short kine and I'm not even sure what kine are." And the Lord produced two stone tablets and snapped them closed on Job's nose. And when Job's wife saw this she wept and the Lord sent an angel of mercy who anointed her head with a polo mallet and of the ten plagues, the Lord sent one through six, inclusive, and Job was sore and his wife angry and she rent her garment and then raised the rent but refused to paint.

And soon Job's pastures dried up and his tongue cleaved to the roof of his mouth so he could not pronounce the word "frankincense" without getting big laughs.

And once the Lord, while wreaking havoc upon his faithful servant, came too close and Job grabbed him around the neck and said, "Aha! Now I got you! Why art thou giving Job a hard time, eh? Eh? Speak up!"

And the Lord said, "Er, look—that's my neck you have . . . Could you let me go?"

But Job showed no mercy and said, "I was doing very well till you came along. I had myrrh and fig trees in abundance and a coat of many colors with two pairs of pants of many colors. Now look."

And the Lord spake and his voice thundered: "Must I who created heaven and earth explain my ways to thee? What hath thou created that thou doth dare question me?"

"That's no answer," Job said. "And for someone who's supposed to be omnipotent, let me tell you, 'tabernacle' has only one *l*." Then Job fell to his knees and cried to the Lord, "Thine is the kingdom and the power and glory. Thou hast a good job. Don't blow it."

Two . . . And Abraham awoke in the middle of the night and said to his only son, Isaac, "I have had an dream where the voice of the Lord sayeth that I must sacrifice my only son, so put your pants on." And Isaac trembled and said, "So what did you say? I mean when He brought this whole thing up?"

"What am I going to say?" Abraham said. "I'm standing there at two A.M. in my underwear with the Creator of the Universe. Should I argue?"

"Well, did he say why he wants me sacrificed?" Isaac asked his father.

But Abraham said, "The faithful do not question. Now let's go because I have a heavy day tomorrow."

And Sarah who heard Abraham's plan grew vexed and said, "How doth thou know it was the Lord and not, say, thy friend who loveth practical jokes, for the Lord hateth practical jokes and whosoever shall pull one shall be delivered into the hands of his enemies whether they can pay the delivery charge or not." And Abraham answered, "Because I know it was the Lord. It was a deep, resonant voice, well modulated, and nobody in the desert can get a rumble in it like that."

And Sarah said, "And thou art willing to carry out this senseless act?" But Abraham told her, "Frankly yes, for to question the Lord's word is one of the worst things a person can do, particularly with the economy in the state it's in."

And so he took Isaac to a certain place and prepared to sacrifice him but at the last minute the Lord stayed Abraham's hand and said, "How could thou doest such a thing?"

And Abraham said, "But thou said—"

"Never mind what I said," the Lord spake. "Doth thou

listen to every crazy idea that comes thy way?" And Abraham grew ashamed. "Er—not really . . . no."

"I jokingly suggest thou sacrifice Isaac and thou immediately runs out to do it."

And Abraham fell to his knees, "See, I never know when you're kidding."

And the Lord thundered, "No sense of humor. I can't believe it."

"But doth this not prove I love thee, that I was willing to donate mine only son on thy whim?"

And the Lord said, "It proves that some men will follow any order no matter how asinine as long as it comes from a resonant, well-modulated voice."

And with that, the Lord bid Abraham get some rest and check with him tomorrow.

Three . . . And it came to pass that a man who sold shirts was smitten by hard times. Neither did any of his merchandise move nor did he prosper. And he prayed and said, "Lord, why hast thou left me to suffer thus? All mine enemies sell their goods except I. And it's the height of the season. My shirts are good shirts. Take a look at this rayon. I got button-downs, flare collars, nothing sells. Yet I have kept thy commandments. Why can I not earn a living when mine younger brother cleans up in children's ready-to-wear?"

And the Lord heard the man and said, "About thy shirts . . ."

"Yes, Lord," the man said, falling to his knees.

"Put an alligator over the pocket."

"Pardon me, Lord?"

"Just do what I'm telling you. You won't be sorry."

And the man sewed on to all his shirts a small alligator symbol and lo and behold, suddenly his merchandise moved like gangbusters, and there was much rejoicing while amongst his enemies there was wailing and gnashing of teeth, and one said, "The Lord is merciful. He maketh me to lie down in green pastures. The problem is, I can't get up."

Laws and Proverbs

· · · · · · · · · · · ·

Doing abominations is against the law, particularly if the abominations are done while wearing a lobster bib.

The lion and the calf shall lie down together but the calf won't get much sleep.

Whosoever shall not fall by the sword or by famine, shall fall by pestilence so why bother shaving?

The wicked at heart probably know something.

Whosoever loveth wisdom is righteous but he that keepeth company with fowl is weird.

My Lord, my Lord! What hast Thou done, lately?

Lovborg's Women Considered

Perhaps no writer has created more fascinating and complex females than the great Scandinavian playwright Jorgen Lovborg, known to his contemporaries as Jorgen Lovborg. Tortured and embittered by his agonizing relationships with the opposite sex, he gave the world such diverse and unforgettable characters as Jenny Angstrom in *Geese Aplenty* and Mrs. Spearing in *A Mother's Gums*. Born in Stockholm in 1836, Lovborg (originally Lövborg, until, in later years, he removed the two dots from above the *o* and placed them over his eyebrows) began writing plays at the age of fourteen. His first produced work, brought to the stage when he was sixty-one, was *Those Who Squirm*, which drew mixed notices from the critics, although the frankness of the subject matter (cheese fondling) caused conservative audiences to blush. Lovborg's work can be divided into three periods. First came the series of plays dealing with anguish, despair, dread, fear, and loneliness (the comedies); the second group focused on social change (Lovborg was instrumental in bringing about safer methods of weighing herring); finally, there were the six great tragedies written just before his death, in Stockholm, in 1902, when his nose fell off, owing to tension.

Lovborg's first outstanding female character was Hedvig Moldau in *I Prefer to Yodel*, the playwright's ironic indictment of penmanship among the upper classes. Hedvig is aware that Greger Norstad has used substandard mortar to roof the henhouse, and when it collapses on Klavar Akdal, causing him to go blind and bald on the same night, she is racked with remorse. The obligatory scene follows:

HEDVIG: So—it collapsed.

DR. RORLUND (*after a long pause*): Yes. It fell down on Akdal's face.

HEDVIG (*ironically*): What was he doing in the henhouse?

DR. RORLUND: He liked the hens. Oh, not all the hens, I'll grant you. But certain ones. (*Significantly*) He had his favorites.

HEDVIG: And Norstad? Where was he during the . . . accident?

DR. RORLUND: He smeared his body with chives and jumped into the reservoir.

HEDVIG (*to herself*): I'll never marry.

DR. RORLUND: What's that?

HEDVIG: Nothing. Come, Doctor. It's time to launder your shorts . . . to launder everybody's shorts. . . .

Hedvig, one of the first really "modern" women, can only sneer when Dr. Rorlund suggests she run up and down in place until Norstad consents to have his hat blocked. She bears close resemblance to Lovborg's own sister Hilda, a neurotic, domineering woman married to a quick-tempered Finnish seaman, who eventually harpooned her. Lovborg worshiped Hilda, and it was her influence that broke him of the habit of speaking to his cane.

The second great "heroine" in Lovborg's work appears in his drama of lust and jealousy *While We Three Hemorrhage*.

Moltvick Dorf, the anchovy trainer, learns that his father's unmentionable disease has been inherited by his brother Eyeowulf. Dorf goes to court, claiming the disease is rightfully his, but Judge Manders upholds Eyeowulf's claim. Netta Holmquist, the beautiful and arrogant actress, tries to persuade Dorf to blackmail Eyeowulf by threatening to tell authorities that he once forged a penguin's signature on some insurance policies. Then, in Act II, Scene 4:

DORF: Oh, Netta. All is lost! Lost!

NETTA: For a weak man, perhaps, but not if one had—courage.

DORF: Courage?

NETTA: To tell Parson Smathers he can never hope to walk again and that for the rest of his life he must skip everywhere.

DORF: Netta! I couldn't!

NETTA: Ha! Of course not! I should have known.

DORF: Parson Smathers trusts Eyeowulf. They shared a piece of chewing gum once. Yes, before I was born. Oh, Netta . . .

NETTA: Stop whining. The bank will never extend the mortgage on Eyeowulf's pretzel. And he's already eaten half of it.

DORF: Netta, what are you suggesting?

NETTA: Nothing a thousand wives would not do for their husbands. I mean to soak Eyeowulf in brine.

DORF: Pickle my own brother?

NETTA: Why not? What do you owe him?

DORF: But such drastic measures! Netta, why not let him keep Father's unmentionable disease? Perhaps we could compromise. Perhaps he would let me have the symptoms.

NETTA: Compromise, ha! Your middle-class mentality makes me sick! Oh, Moltvick, I'm so bored by this marriage! Bored by your ideas, your ways, your conversations. And your habit of wearing feathers to dinner.

DORF: Oh! Not my feathers, too!

NETTA (*contemptuously*): I am going to tell you something now that only I and your mother know. You are a dwarf.

DORF: *What?*

NETTA: Everything in the house has been made to scale. You are only forty-eight inches tall.

DORF: Don't, don't! The pains are returning!

NETTA: Yes, Moltvick!

DORF: My kneecaps—they're throbbing!

NETTA: What a weakling.

DORF: Netta, Netta, open the shutters . . .

NETTA: I'll close them.

DORF: Light! Moltvick needs light . . .

To Lovborg, Moltvick represented the old, decadent, dying Europe. Netta, on the other hand, was the new—the vibrant, cruel Darwinian force of nature, which was to blow through Europe for the next fifty years and find its deepest expression in the songs of Maurice Chevalier. The relationship between Netta and Moltvick mirrored Lovborg's marriage to Siri Brackman, an actress who served as a constant inspiration to him throughout the eight hours their marriage lasted. Lovborg remarried several times after that, but always to department-store mannequins.

Clearly, the most fully realized woman in all of Lovborg's plays was Mrs. Sanstad in *Mellow Pears*, Lovborg's last naturalistic drama. (After *Pears*, he experimented with an Expressionist play in which all the characters were named Lovborg, but it failed to win approval, and for the remaining three years of his life he could not be coaxed out of the hamper.) *Mellow Pears* ranks with his greatest works, and the final exchange between Mrs. Sanstad and her son's wife, Berte, is perhaps more pertinent today than ever:

BERTE: Do say you like the way we furnished the house! It was so hard, on a ventriloquist's salary.

MRS. SANSTAD: The house is—serviceable.

BERTE: What! Only serviceable?

MRS. SANSTAD: Whose idea was the red satin elk?

BERTE: Why, your son's. Henrick is a born decorator.

MRS. SANSTAD (*suddenly*): Henrick is a fool!

BERTE: No!

MRS. SANSTAD: Did you know that he did not know what snow was until last week?

BERTE: You're lying!

MRS. SANSTAD: My precious son. Yes, Henrick—the same man who went to prison for mispronouncing the word "diphthong."

BERTE: No!

MRS. SANSTAD: Yes. And with an Eskimo in the room at the time!

BERTE: I don't want to hear about it!

MRS. SANSTAD: But you will, my little nightingale! Isn't that what Henrick calls you?

BERTE (*crying*): He calls me nightingale! Yes, and sometimes thrush! And hippo!

(*Both women weep unashamedly.*)

MRS. SANSTAD: Berte, dear Berte! . . . Henrick's earmuffs are not his own! They are owned by a corporation.

BERTE: We must help him. He must be told he can never fly by flapping his arms.

MRS. SANSTAD (*suddenly laughing*): Henrick knows everything. I told him your feelings about his arch supports.

BERTE: So! You tricked me!

MRS. SANSTAD: Call it what you will. He's in Oslo now.

BERTE: Oslo!

MRS. SANSTAD: With his geranium . . .

BERTE: I see. I . . . see. (*She wanders through the French doors upstage.*)

MRS. SANSTAD: Yes, my little nightingale, he is out of your clutches at last. By this time next month, he will realize his lifelong dream—to fill his hat with cinders. And you thought you'd keep him cooped up here! No! Henrick is a wild creature, a thing of nature! Like some wonderful mouse—or a tick. (*A shot is heard. Mrs. Sanstad runs into the next room. We hear a scream. She returns, pale and shaken.*) Dead . . . She's lucky. I . . . must go on. Yes, night is falling . . . falling rapidly. So rapidly, and I still have all those chickpeas to rearrange.

Mrs. Sanstad was Lovborg's revenge on his mother. Also a critical woman, she began life as a trapeze artist with the circus; his father, Nils Lovborg, was the human cannonball. The two met in midair and were married before touching ground. Bitterness slowly crept into the marriage, and by the time Lovborg was six years old his parents exchanged gunfire daily. This atmosphere took its toll on a sensitive youngster like Jorgen, and soon he began to suffer the first of his famous "moods" and "anxieties," rendering him for some years unable to pass a roast chicken without tipping his hat. In later years, he told friends that he was tense all during the writing of *Mellow Pears* and on several occasions believed he heard his mother's voice asking him directions to Staten Island.

The Whore of Mensa

One thing about being a private investigator, you've got to learn to go with your hunches. That's why when a quivering pat of butter named Word Babcock walked into my office and laid his cards on the table, I should have trusted the cold chill that shot up my spine.

"Kaiser?" he said. "Kaiser Lupowitz?"

"That's what it says on my license," I owned up.

"You've got to help me. I'm being blackmailed. Please!"

He was shaking like the lead singer in a rumba band. I pushed a glass across the desk top and a bottle of rye I keep handy for nonmedicinal purposes. "Suppose you relax and tell me all about it."

"You . . . you won't tell my wife?"

"Level with me, Word. I can't make any promises."

He tried pouring a drink, but you could hear the clicking sound across the street, and most of the stuff wound up in his shoes.

"I'm a working guy," he said. "Mechanical maintenance. I build and service joy buzzers. You know—those little fun gimmicks that give people a shock when they shake hands?"

"So?"

"A lot of your executives like 'em. Particularly down on Wall Street."

"Get to the point."

"I'm on the road a lot. You know how it is—lonely. Oh, not what you're thinking. See, Kaiser, I'm basically an intellectual. Sure, a guy can meet all the bimbos he wants. But the really brainy women—they're not so easy to find on short notice."

"Keep talking."

"Well, I heard of this young girl. Eighteen years old. A Vassar student. For a price, she'll come over and discuss any subject—Proust, Yeats, anthropology. Exchange of ideas. You see what I'm driving at?"

"Not exactly."

"I mean, my wife is great, don't get me wrong. But she won't discuss Pound with me. Or Eliot. I didn't know that when I married her. See, I need a woman who's mentally stimulating, Kaiser. And I'm willing to pay for it. I don't want an involvement—I want a quick intellectual experience, then I want the girl to leave. Christ, Kaiser, I'm a happily married man."

"How long has this been going on?"

"Six months. Whenever I have that craving, I call Flossie. She's a madam, with a master's in comparative lit. She sends me over an intellectual, see?"

So he was one of those guys whose weakness was really bright women. I felt sorry for the poor sap. I figured there must be a lot of jokers in his position, who were starved for a little intellectual communication with the opposite sex and would pay through the nose for it.

"Now she's threatening to tell my wife," he said.

"Who is?"

"Flossie. They bugged the motel room. They got tapes of me discussing *The Waste Land* and *Styles of Radical Will*, and, well, really getting into some issues. They want ten grand or they go to Carla. Kaiser, you've got to help me! Carla would die if she knew she didn't turn me on up here."

The old call-girl racket. I had heard rumors that the boys at headquarters were on to something involving a group of educated women, but so far they were stymied.

"Get Flossie on the phone for me."

"What?"

"I'll take your case, Word. But I get fifty dollars a day, plus expenses. You'll have to repair a lot of joy buzzers."

"It won't be ten Gs' worth, I'm sure of that," he said with a grin, and picked up the phone and dialed a number. I took it from him and winked. I was beginning to like him.

Seconds later, a silky voice answered, and I told her what was on my mind. "I understand you can help me set up an hour of good chat," I said.

"Sure, honey. What do you have in mind?"

"I'd like to discuss Melville."

"*Moby Dick* or the shorter novels?"

"What's the difference?"

"The price. That's all. Symbolism's extra."

"What'll it run me?"

"Fifty, maybe a hundred for *Moby Dick*. You want a comparative discussion—Melville and Hawthorne? That could be arranged for a hundred."

"The dough's fine," I told her and gave her the number of a room at the Plaza.

"You want a blonde or a brunette?"

"Surprise me," I said, and hung up.

I shaved and grabbed some black coffee while I checked over the Monarch College Outline series. Hardly an hour had passed before there was a knock on my door. I opened it, and standing there was a young redhead who was packed into her slacks like two big scoops of vanilla ice cream.

"Hi, I'm Sherry."

They really knew how to appeal to your fantasies. Long straight hair, leather bag, silver earrings, no make-up.

"I'm surprised you weren't stopped, walking into the

hotel dressed like that," I said. "The house dick can usually spot an intellectual."

"A five-spot cools him."

"Shall we begin?" I said, motioning her to the couch.

She lit a cigarette and got right to it. "I think we could start by approaching *Billy Budd* as Melville's justification of the ways of God to man, *n'est-ce pas?*"

"Interestingly, though, not in a Miltonian sense." I was bluffing. I wanted to see if she'd go for it.

"No. *Paradise Lost* lacked the substructure of pessimism." She did.

"Right, right. God, you're right," I murmured.

"I think Melville reaffirmed the virtues of innocence in a naïve yet sophisticated sense—don't you agree?"

I let her go on. She was barely nineteen years old, but already she had developed the hardened facility of the pseudo-intellectual. She rattled off her ideas glibly, but it was all mechanical. Whenever I offered an insight, she faked a response: "Oh, yes, Kaiser. Yes, baby, that's deep. A platonic comprehension of Christianity—why didn't I see it before?"

We talked for about an hour and then she said she had to go. She stood up and I laid a C-note on her.

"Thanks, honey."

"There's plenty more where that came from."

"What are you trying to say?"

I had piqued her curiosity. She sat down again.

"Suppose I wanted to—have a party?" I said.

"Like, what kind of party?"

"Suppose I wanted Noam Chomsky explained to me by two girls?"

"Oh, wow."

"If you'd rather forget it . . ."

"You'd have to speak with Flossie," she said. "It'd cost you."

Now was the time to tighten the screws. I flashed my

private-investigator's badge and informed her it was a bust.

"What!"

"I'm fuzz, sugar, and discussing Melville for money is an 802. You can do time."

"You louse!"

"Better come clean, baby. Unless you want to tell your story down at Alfred Kazin's office, and I don't think he'd be too happy to hear it."

She began to cry. "Don't turn me in, Kaiser," she said. "I needed the money to complete my master's. I've been turned down for a grant. *Twice*. Oh, Christ."

It all poured out—the whole story. Central Park West upbringing, Socialist summer camps, Brandeis. She was every dame you saw waiting in line at the Elgin or the Thalia, or penciling the words "Yes, very true" into the margin of some book on Kant. Only somewhere along the line she had made a wrong turn.

"I needed cash. A girl friend said she knew a married guy whose wife wasn't very profound. He was into Blake. She couldn't hack it. I said sure, for a price I'd talk Blake with him. I was nervous at first. I faked a lot of it. He didn't care. My friend said there were others. Oh, I've been busted before. I got caught reading *Commentary* in a parked car, and I was once stopped and frisked at Tanglewood. Once more and I'm a three-time loser."

"Then take me to Flossie."

She bit her lip and said, "The Hunter College Book Store is a front."

"Yes?"

"Like those bookie joints that have barbershops outside for show. You'll see."

I made a quick call to headquarters and then said to her, "Okay, sugar. You're off the hook. But don't leave town."

She tilted her face up toward mine gratefully. "I can get you photographs of Dwight Macdonald reading," she said.

"Some other time."

I walked into the Hunter College Book Store. The salesman, a young man with sensitive eyes, came up to me. "Can I help you?" he said.

"I'm looking for a special edition of *Advertisements for Myself*. I understand the author had several thousand gold-leaf copies printed up for friends."

"I'll have to check," he said. "We have a WATS line to Mailer's house."

I fixed him with a look. "Sherry sent me," I said.

"Oh, in that case, go on back," he said. He pressed a button. A wall of books opened, and I walked like a lamb into that bustling pleasure palace known as Flossie's.

Red flocked wallpaper and a Victorian décor set the tone. Pale, nervous girls with black-rimmed glasses and blunt-cut hair lolled around on sofas, riffling Penguin Classics provocatively. A blonde with a big smile winked at me, nodded toward a room upstairs, and said, "Wallace Stevens, eh?" But it wasn't just intellectual experiences—they were peddling emotional ones, too. For fifty bucks, I learned, you could "relate without getting close." For a hundred, a girl would lend you her Bartók records, have dinner, and then let you watch while she had an anxiety attack. For one-fifty, you could listen to FM radio with twins. For three bills, you got the works: A thin Jewish brunette would pretend to pick you up at the Museum of Modern Art, let you read her master's, get you involved in a screaming quarrel at Elaine's over Freud's conception of women, and then fake a suicide of your choosing—the perfect evening, for some guys. Nice racket. Great town, New York.

"Like what you see?" a voice said behind me. I turned and suddenly found myself standing face to face with the business end of a .38. I'm a guy with a strong stomach, but this time it did a back flip. It was Flossie, all right. The voice was the same, but Flossie was a man. His face was hidden by a mask.

"You'll never believe this," he said, "but I don't even have a college degree. I was thrown out for low grades."

"Is that why you wear that mask?"

"I devised a complicated scheme to take over *The New York Review of Books*, but it meant I had to pass for Lionel Trilling. I went to Mexico for an operation. There's a doctor in Juarez who gives people Trilling's features—for a price. Something went wrong. I came out looking like Auden, with Mary McCarthy's voice. That's when I started working the other side of the law."

Quickly, before he could tighten his finger on the trigger, I went into action. Heaving forward, I snapped my elbow across his jaw and grabbed the gun as he fell back. He hit the ground like a ton of bricks. He was still whimpering when the police showed up.

"Nice work, Kaiser," Sergeant Holmes said. "When we're through with this guy, the F.B.I. wants to have a talk with him. A little matter involving some gamblers and an annotated copy of Dante's *Inferno*. Take him away, boys."

Later that night, I looked up an old account of mine named Gloria. She was blond. She had graduated *cum laude*. The difference was she majored in physical education. It felt good.

Death

. . . .

A PLAY

The curtain rises on KLEINMAN, asleep in his bed at two A.M.
There is a pounding at the door. Finally, and with great effort and
determination, he gets up.

KLEINMAN

Huh?

VOICES

Open up! Hey—come on, we know you're there! Open up!
Let's go, open! . . .

KLEINMAN

Huh? What?

VOICES

Let's go, open up!

KLEINMAN

What? Wait! *(Turns on the light)* Who's there?

VOICES

Come on, open up! Let's go!

KLEINMAN

Who is it?

VOICE

Let's go, Kleinman—hurry.

KLEINMAN

Hacker—that's Hacker's voice. Hacker?

VOICE

Kleinman, will you open up?!

KLEINMAN

I'm coming, I'm coming. I was asleep—wait! *(All with stumbling and great effort and clumsiness. He looks at the clock)* My God, it's two-thirty . . . Coming, wait a minute! *(He opens the door and a half-dozen men enter)*

HANK

For God's sake, Kleinman, are you deaf?

KLEINMAN

I was asleep. It's two-thirty. What's going on?

AL

We need you. Get dressed.

KLEINMAN

What?

SAM

Let's go, Kleinman. We don't have forever.

KLEINMAN

What is this?

AL

Come on, move.

KLEINMAN

Move where? Hacker, it's the middle of the night.

HACKER

Well, wake up.

KLEINMAN

What's going on?

JOHN

Don't play ignorant.

KLEINMAN

Who's playing ignorant? I was in a deep sleep. What do you think I was doing two-thirty in the morning—dancing?

HACKER

We need every available man.

KLEINMAN

For what?

VICTOR

What's wrong with you, Kleinman? Where have you been that you don't know what's going on?

KLEINMAN

What are you talking about?

AL

Vigilantes.

KLEINMAN

What?

AL

Vigilantes.

JOHN

But with a plan this time.

HACKER

And well worked out.

SAM

A great plan.

KLEINMAN

Er, does anybody want to tell me why you're here? Because I'm cold in my underwear.

HACKER

Let's just say we need all the help we can get. Now get dressed.

VICTOR
(Menacingly)
And hurry.

KLEINMAN
Okay, I'm getting dressed . . . May I please know what it's all about?
(He starts pulling on some trousers apprehensively)

JOHN
The killer's been spotted. By two women. They saw him entering the park.

KLEINMAN
What killer?

VICTOR
Kleinman, this is no time for babbling.

KLEINMAN
Who's babbling? What killer? You come barging in—I'm in a deep sleep—

HACKER
Richardson's killer—Jampel's killer.

AL
Mary Quilty's killer.

SAM
The maniac.

HANK
The strangler.

KLEINMAN
Which maniac? Which strangler?

JOHN
The same one who killed Eisler's boy and strangled Jensen with piano wire.

KLEINMAN

Jensen? . . . The big night watchman?

HACKER

That's right. He took him from behind. Crept up quietly
and slipped piano wire around his neck. He was blue when
they found him. Saliva frozen down the corner of his mouth.

KLEINMAN
(Looks around the room)
Yeah, well, look, I have to go to work tomorrow—

VICTOR

Let's go, Kleinman. We've got to stop him before he strikes
again.

Kleinman

We? We and me?

HACKER

The police can't seem to handle it.

KLEINMAN

Well, then we should write letters and complain. I'll get on
it first thing in the morning.

HACKER

They're doing the best they can, Kleinman. They're
baffled.

SAM

Everyone's baffled.

AL

Don't tell us you've heard nothing about all this?

JOHN

That's hard to believe.

KLEINMAN

Well, the truth is—it's the height of the season . . . We're
busy . . . *(They're not buying his naïveté)* Don't even take a

lunch hour—and I love to eat . . . Hacker'll tell you I love to eat.

HACKER

But this ghastly business has been going on for some time now. Don't you follow the news?

KLEINMAN

I don't get a chance.

HACKER

Everyone's terrified. People can't walk the streets at night.

JOHN

Streets nothing. The Simon sisters were killed in their own home because they didn't lock the door. Throats cut ear to ear.

KLEINMAN

I thought you said he's a strangler.

JOHN

Kleinman, don't be naïve.

KLEINMAN

N–now that you mention it, I could use a new lock on this door.

HACKER

It's horrible. No one knows when he'll strike next.

KLEINMAN

When did it start? I don't know why I wasn't told anything.

HACKER

First one body, then another, then more. The city's in a panic. Everyone but you.

KLEINMAN

Well, you can relax, because now I'm in a panic.

HACKER

It's difficult in the case of a madman because there's no motive. Nothing to go on.

KLEINMAN

No one's been robbed or raped or—tickled a little?

VICTOR

Only strangled.

KLEINMAN

Even Jensen . . . He's so powerful.

SAM

He *was* powerful. Right now, his tongue is sticking out and he's blue.

KLEINMAN

Blue . . . It's a bad color for a man of forty . . . And there's no clue? A hair—or a fingerprint?

HACKER

Yes. They found a hair.

KLEINMAN

So? All they need today is one hair. Put it under a microscope. One, two, three, they know the whole story. What color is it?

HACKER

Your color.

KLEINMAN

My—don't look at me . . . Nothing of mine's fallen out recently. I . . . Look, let's not get crazy . . . The trick is to remain logical.

HACKER

Uh-huh.

KLEINMAN

Sometimes there's a clue in the victims—like they're all nurses or they're all bald . . . or bald nurses . . .

JOHN

You tell us what the similarity is?

SAM

That's right. Between Eisler's boy and Mary Quilty and Jensen and Jampel—

KLEINMAN

If I knew more about the case . . .

AL

If he knew more about the case. There *is* no similarity. Except once they all were alive and now they're all dead. There's the thing in common.

HACKER

He's right. No one is safe, Kleinman. If that's what you're thinking.

AL

He probably wants to reassure himself!

JOHN

Yeah.

SAM

There is no pattern, Kleinman.

VICTOR

It's not just nurses.

AL

No one's immune.

KLEINMAN

I wasn't trying to reassure myself. I was asking a simple question.

SAM

Well, don't ask so many damn questions. We've got work to
do.

VICTOR

We're all worried. Anyone can be next.

KLEINMAN

Look, I'm not good at these things. What do I know about a
manhunt? I'll just be in the way. Let me make a cash
donation. That'll be my contribution. Let me pledge a few
dollars—

SAM
(Finding a hair by the bureau)

What's this?

KLEINMAN

What?

SAM

This? In your comb. It's a hair.

KLEINMAN

That's because I use it to comb my hair.

SAM

The color's identical with the hair found by the police.

KLEINMAN

Are you crazy? It's a black hair. There's a million of black
hairs around. Why are you putting it in an envelope?
Wha—it's a common thing. Here—*(Points to JOHN)* him—
he's got black hair.

JOHN
(Grabs KLEINMAN)

What are you accusing me of, eh, Kleinman?!

KLEINMAN

Who's accusing!? He's got my hair in an envelope. Give me that hair back!
(Grabs the envelope, but JOHN pulls him off)

JOHN

Leave him alone!

SAM

I'm doing my duty.

VICTOR

He's right. The police have requested all citizens' help.

HACKER

Yes. Now we have a plan.

KLEINMAN

What kind of plan?

AL

We can count on you, can't we?

VICTOR

Oh, we can count on Kleinman. He figures in the plan.

KLEINMAN

I do figure in the plan? So what's the plan?

JOHN

You'll be informed, don't worry.

KLEINMAN

He needs my hair in that envelope?

SAM

Just get your clothes on and meet us downstairs. And hurry up. We're wasting time.

KLEINMAN

Okay, but give me a hint what the plan is like?

HACKER

Hurry, Kleinman, for God's sake. This is a matter of life
and death. You better dress warm. It's cold out there.

KLEINMAN

Okay, okay . . . just tell me the plan. If I know the plan I
can think about it.
*(But they go, leaving KLEINMAN to dress with a nervous
clumsiness)*

KLEINMAN

Where the hell's my shoehorn? . . . This is ridiculous . . .
wake a man up in the middle of the night and with such
horrible news. What are we paying a police force for? One
minute I'm curled up asleep in a nice warm bed and the
next I'm involved in some plan, a homicidal maniac who
comes up behind you and—

ANNA

*(An old battle-ax, enters with candle, unseen, surprising KLEIN-
MAN)* Kleinman?

KLEINMAN
(Turning, frightened out of his wits)
Who's that!!?

ANNA

What?

KLEINMAN

For God's sake, don't creep up on me like that!

ANNA

I heard voices.

KLEINMAN

Some men were here. All of a sudden I'm on a vigilante
committee.

ANNA

Now?

KLEINMAN

Apparently there's a killer loose—it can't wait for the morning. He's a night owl.

ANNA

Oh, the maniac.

KLEINMAN

So if you knew about it, why didn't you tell me?

ANNA

Because everytime I try and talk to you about it you don't want to hear.

KLEINMAN

Who doesn't?

ANNA

You're always too busy with work—and your hobbies.

KLEINMAN

Do you mind if it's the height of the season?

ANNA

I said to you there's an unsolved murder, there's two unsolved murders, there's six unsolved murders—and all you say is, "Later, later."

KLEINMAN

Because the times you pick to tell me.

ANNA

Yeah?

KLEINMAN

My birthday party. So I'm having a good time, I'm opening presents, so you creep up to me with that long face and say, "Did you read in the paper? A girl got her throat cut?" You couldn't pick a more appropriate time? A man has a little fun—enter the voice of doom.

ANNA

Unless it's something nice, no time is appropriate.

KLEINMAN

Meanwhile, where's my tie?

ANNA

What do you need a tie for? You're going to hunt a maniac?

KLEINMAN

Do you mind?

ANNA

What is it, a formal hunt?

KLEINMAN

Do I know who I'm going to meet? What if my boss is down there?

ANNA

I'm sure he's dressed casually.

KLEINMAN

Look who they're enlisting to track down a killer. I'm a salesman.

ANNA

Don't let him get behind you.

KLEINMAN

Thanks, Anna, I'll tell him you said to keep in front.

ANNA

Well, you don't have to be so nasty. He's got to be caught.

KLEINMAN

Then let the police catch him. I'm scared to go down there. It's cold and dark.

ANNA

Be a man for once in your life.

KLEINMAN

That's easy for you to say, because you're going back to bed.

ANNA

And what if he should find his way to this house and come in a window?

KLEINMAN

Then you got problems.

ANNA

If I'm attacked, I'll blow pepper on him.

KLEINMAN

Blow what?

ANNA

I sleep with a little pepper near the bed, and if he comes near me I'll blow pepper in his eyes.

KLEINMAN

Good thinking, Anna. Believe me, if he gets in here, you and your pepper will be on the ceiling.

ANNA

I'm keeping everything double-locked.

KLEINMAN

Hm, maybe I better take some pepper.

ANNA

Take this.
(She hands him a charm)

KLEINMAN

What's this?

ANNA

A charm that wards off evil. I bought it from a crippled beggar.

KLEINMAN
(Looks at it, unimpressed)
Right. Just give me some pepper.

ANNA
Oh, don't worry. You won't be alone down there.

KLEINMAN
That's true. They've got a very clever plan.

ANNA
What?

KLEINMAN
I don't know yet.

ANNA
So how do you know it's so clever?

KLEINMAN
Because these are the best minds in town. Believe me, they
know what they're doing.

ANNA
I hope so, for your sake.

KLEINMAN
All right, keep the door locked and don't open it for
anyone—not even me, unless I happen to be screaming,
"Open the door!" Then open it quickly.

ANNA
Good luck, Kleinman.

KLEINMAN
(Takes a look out his window into the black night)
Look at it out there . . . It's so black . . .

ANNA
I don't see anybody.

KLEINMAN

Me neither. You'd figure there'd be groups of citizens with torches or something—

ANNA

Well, as long as they've got a plan.
(*Pause*)

KLEINMAN

Anna—

ANNA

Yes?

KLEINMAN
(*Looking into the black*)
Do you ever think of dying?

ANNA

Why should I think of dying? Why, do you?

KLEINMAN

Not usually, but when I do, it's not by being strangled or having my throat cut.

ANNA

I should hope not.

KLEINMAN

I think of dying in a nicer way.

ANNA

Believe me, there's plenty of nicer ways.

KLEINMAN

Like what?

ANNA

Like what? You're asking me a nice way to die?

KLEINMAN

Yeah.

ANNA

I'm thinking.

KLEINMAN

Yeah.

ANNA

Poison.

KLEINMAN

Poison? That's terrible.

ANNA

Why?

KLEINMAN

Are you joking? You get cramps.

ANNA

Not necessarily.

KLEINMAN

Do you know what you're talking about?

ANNA

Potassium cyanide.

KLEINMAN

Oh . . . my expert. You're not catching me with poison. You know what it is even if you eat a bad clam?

ANNA

That's not poison. That's food poisoning.

KLEINMAN

Who wants to swallow anything?

ANNA

So how do you want to die?

KLEINMAN

Old age. Many years in the future. When I'm through the

long journey of life. Surrounded in a comfortable bed by
relatives—when I'm ninety.

ANNA

But that's just a dream. Obviously, at any second you could
get your neck snapped in two by a homicidal killer—or
your throat cut . . . not when you're ninety, right now.

KLEINMAN

It's so comforting to discuss these things with you, Anna.

ANNA

Well, I'm worried about you. Look at it down there. There's
a killer loose and plenty of places to hide on such a black
night—alleys, doorways, under the railroad overpass . . .
You'd never see him in a dark shadow—a diseased mind,
lurking in the night with piano wire—

KLEINMAN

You made your point—I'm going back to bed!
(*Knock on door and voice*)

VOICE

Let's go, Kleinman!

KLEINMAN

I'm coming, I'm coming. (*Kisses ANNA*) See you later.

ANNA

Look where you're going.
(*He goes out, joining AL, who has been left to see that he gets things
straight*)

KLEINMAN

I don't know why this is suddenly my responsibility.

AL

We're all in it together.

KLEINMAN

It'll be just my luck, I'll be the one to find him. Oh, I forgot my pepper!

AL

What?

KLEINMAN

Hey, where is everybody?

AL

They had to move on. Correct timing is urgent in bringing the plan off.

KLEINMAN

So what is this great plan?

AL

You'll find out.

KLEINMAN

When are you going to tell me? After he's captured?

AL

Don't be so impatient.

KLEINMAN

Look—it's late, and I'm cold. Not to mention nervous.

AL

Hacker and the others had to leave, but he said to tell you you'll receive word as soon as possible as to how you fit in.

KLEINMAN

Hacker said that?

AL

Yes.

KLEINMAN

So what do I do, now that I'm out of my room and my warm bed?

AL

You wait.

KLEINMAN

For what?

AL

For word.

KLEINMAN

What word?

AL

Word of how you fit in.

KLEINMAN

I'm going back home.

AL

No! Don't you dare. A wrong move at this point could endanger all our lives. You think I want to wind up a corpse?

KLEINMAN

So tell me the plan.

AL

I can't tell you.

KLEINMAN

Why not?

AL

Because I don't know it.

KLEINMAN

Look, it's a cold night—

AL

Each of us only knows one small fraction of the overall plan at any given moment—his own assignment—and no one is allowed to disclose his function to another. It's a precaution against the maniac finding out the plan. If each man properly brings off his own part, then the whole scheme will be brought to a successful conclusion. In the meantime, the plan can't be either carelessly disclosed or given up under duress or threat. Each one can only account for a tiny fragment which would have no meaning to the maniac should he gain access to it. Clever?

KLEINMAN

Brilliant. I don't know what's going on and I'm going home.

AL

I can't say any more. Suppose it was you who killed all those people?

KLEINMAN

Me?

AL

The killer might be any of us.

KLEINMAN

Well, it's not me. I don't go around hacking people to death at the height of the season.

AL

I'm sorry, Kleinman.

KLEINMAN

So what do I do? What's my assignment?

AL

If I were you I would try and contribute as best I could until my function became clearer.

KLEINMAN

Contribute how?

AL

It's hard to be specific.

KLEINMAN

Can you give me a hint? Because I'm beginning to feel like a fool.

AL

Things may seem chaotic but they're not.

KLEINMAN

But there was such a rush to get me out here. Now I'm here and ready and everybody's gone.

AL

I have to go.

KLEINMAN

So what was so urgent? . . . Go? What do you mean?

AL

My work is finished here. I'm due elsewhere.

KLEINMAN

That means I'll be out here on the street myself.

AL

Perhaps.

KLEINMAN

Perhaps nothing. If we're together and you leave, I'm alone. That's arithmetic.

AL

Be careful.

KLEINMAN

Oh, no, I'm not staying here alone! You gotta be kidding! There's a madman walking around loose! I don't get along with madmen! I'm a very logical guy.

AL

The plan doesn't allow for us to be together.

KLEINMAN

Look, let's not make it into a romance. *We* don't have to be together. Me and any twelve strong men will do.

AL

I must go.

KLEINMAN

I don't want to be here alone. I'm serious.

AL

Just be careful.

KLEINMAN

Look, my hand is shaking—and you haven't left yet! You go and my whole body'll shake.

AL

Kleinman, other lives are dependent on you. Don't fail us.

KLEINMAN

You shouldn't count on me. I have a great fear of death! I'd rather do almost anything else than die!

AL

Good luck.

KLEINMAN

And what about the maniac? Is there any further news? Has he been spotted again?

AL

The police saw a large, terrifying figure lurking near the ice company. But no one really knows.
(Exits. We hear his footsteps going off softer and softer)

KLEINMAN

It's enough for me! I'll stay away from the ice company! *(Alone—wind sound effects)* Oh, boy, nothing like a night on the town. I don't know why I can't just wait in my room till I'm given a specific assignment. What was that noise!? The

wind—the wind is not too thrilling either. It could blow a
sign down on me. Well, I've got to keep calm . . . People
are counting on me . . . Keep my eyes open and if I see
something suspicious I'll report it to the others . . . Except
there are no others . . . I have to remember to make some
more friends next chance I get . . . Maybe if I walked up a
block or two I'll run into some of the others . . . How far
could they have gotten? Unless this is what they want.
Maybe this is part of the scheme. Maybe if anything
dangerous happens, Hacker has me under some kind of
surveillance where they'd all come to my aid . . . *(Laughs
nervously)* I'm sure I haven't been left alone to wander the
streets all by myself. They have to realize I'd be no match
for a crazy killer. A maniac has the strength of ten and I
have the strength of a half of one . . . Unless they're using
me as a decoy . . . You think they'd do that? Leave me out
here like a lamb? . . . The killer pounces on me and they
come bursting out quickly and grab him—unless they come
bursting out slowly . . . I never had a strong neck. *(A black
figure runs across background)* What was that? Maybe I should
go back . . . I'm starting to get far from where I started
. . . How are they going to find me to assign me my
instructions? Not only that, but I'm going toward a part of
the city which is unfamiliar to me . . . then what?
Yeah—maybe I better turn around and retrace my steps
before I become good and lost . . . *(He hears slow, menacing
steps coming toward him)* Uh-oh . . . That's footsteps—the
maniac probably has feet . . . Oh, God, save me . . .

DOCTOR

Kleinman, is that you?

KLEINMAN

What? Who is it?

DOCTOR

It's just the doctor.

KLEINMAN

You gave me a scare. Tell me, have you heard anything
from Hacker or any of the others?

DOCTOR

Concerning your participation?

KLEINMAN

Yes. Time is being wasted and I'm wandering around like a
jackass. I mean, I'm keeping my eyes open, but if I knew
what I was supposed to be doing—

DOCTOR

Hacker did mention something about you.

KLEINMAN

What?

DOCTOR

I can't remember.

KLEINMAN

Great. I'm the forgotten man.

DOCTOR

I think I heard him say something. I'm not sure.

KLEINMAN

Look, why don't we patrol together? In case there's trouble.

DOCTOR

I can only walk along a little way with you. Then I have
other business.

KLEINMAN

It's funny to see a doctor up in the middle of the night . . . I
know how you guys hate to make house calls. Ha-ha-ha-ha.
(No laugh) It's a very cold night . . . *(Nothing)* You, er—you
think we'll spot him tonight? *(Nothing)* I suppose you have
an important function to carry out in the plan? See, I don't
know mine yet.

DOCTOR

My interest is purely scientific.

KLEINMAN

I'm sure.

DOCTOR

Here is a chance to learn something about the nature of his insanity. Why is he the way he is? What goads someone toward such a type of antisocial behavior? Are there some other unusual qualities about him? Sometimes the very impulses that cause a maniac to murder inspire him to highly creative ends. It's a very complex phenomenon. Also, I would like to know if he has been mad from birth or if his madness is caused by some disease or accident that has damaged his brain or from the accumulated stress of adverse circumstances. There are a million facts to learn. For instance: Why does he choose to express his impulses in the act of murder? Does he do it of his own will or does he imagine he hears voices? You know at one time the mad were considered to be divinely inspired. All this is worth examining for the record.

KLEINMAN

Sure, but first we have to catch him.

DOCTOR

Yes, Kleinman, if I have my way, I will be left alone to study this creature scrupulously, dissecting him down to the last chromosome. I would like to put his every cell under a microscope. See what he's composed of. Analyze his juices. Break down the blood, probe the brain minutely, until I had a one hundred percent understanding of precisely what he is in every aspect.

KLEINMAN

Can you ever really know a person? I mean, know him—not know about him, but know—I mean, actually

know him—where you know him—I'm talking about
knowing a person—you know what I mean by knowing?
Knowing. Really knowing. To know. Know. To know.

DOCTOR

Kleinman, you're an idiot.

KLEINMAN

Do you understand what I'm saying?

DOCTOR

You do your job and I'll do mine.

KLEINMAN

I don't know my job.

DOCTOR

Then don't criticize.

KLEINMAN

Who's criticizing? *(A scream is heard. They start)* What was
that?

DOCTOR

Do you hear footsteps behind us?

KLEINMAN

I've been hearing footsteps behind me since I was eight
years old.

(Scream again)

DOCTOR

Someone's coming.

KLEINMAN

Maybe he didn't like all that talk about dissecting him.

DOCTOR

You'd better get out of here, Kleinman.

KLEINMAN

My pleasure.

DOCTOR

Quick! This way!
(Noise of someone approaching heavily)

KLEINMAN

That alley's a dead end.

DOCTOR

I know what I'm doing!

KLEINMAN

Yeah, but we'll be trapped and killed!

DOCTOR

Are you going to argue with me? I'm a doctor.

KLEINMAN

But I know that alley—it's a dead end. There's no way of getting out!

DOCTOR

Goodbye, Kleinman. Do what you want!
(He runs up the dead end)

KLEINMAN
(Calling after him)

Wait—I'm sorry! *(Noise of someone approaching)* I've got to stay calm! Do I run or do I hide? I'll run and hide! *(He runs and bumps into a young WOMAN)* Oooof!

GINA

Oh!

KLEINMAN

Who are you?

GINA

Who are you?

KLEINMAN

Kleinman. Did you hear screams?

GINA

Yes, and I got scared. I don't know where they were coming from.

KLEINMAN

It doesn't matter. The main thing is that they were screams, and screams are never any good.

GINA

I'm frightened!

KLEINMAN

Let's get out of here!

GINA

I can't go too far. I have something to do.

KLEINMAN

You're in on the plan too?

GINA

Aren't you?

KLEINMAN

Not yet. I can't seem to find out what I should be doing. You haven't heard anything about me by any chance?

GINA

You're Kleinman.

KLEINMAN

Exactly.

GINA

I heard something about a Kleinman. I don't remember what.

KLEINMAN

You know where Hacker is?

GINA

Hacker was murdered.

KLEINMAN

What!?

GINA

I think it was Hacker.

KLEINMAN

Hacker's dead?

GINA

I'm not sure if they said Hacker or someone else.

KLEINMAN

Nobody's sure of anything! Nobody knows anything! This is some plan! We're dropping like flies!

GINA

Maybe it wasn't Hacker.

KLEINMAN

Let's get away from here. I wandered away from where I should have been, and they're probably looking for me, and with my luck, they'll blame me if the plan fails.

GINA

I can't remember who's dead. Hacker or Maxwell.

KLEINMAN

I'll tell you the truth, it's hard to keep track. And what's a young woman like yourself doing out on the streets? This is a man's work.

GINA

I'm used to the streets at night.

KLEINMAN

Oh?

GINA

Well, I'm a prostitute.

KLEINMAN

No kidding. Gee, I never met one before . . . I thought
you'd be taller.

GINA

I didn't embarrass you, did I?

KLEINMAN

To tell you the truth, I'm very provincial.

GINA

Yes?

KLEINMAN

I, er—I'm never even up at this hour. I mean *never.* It's the
middle of the night. Unless I'm sick or something—but
barring extreme nausea I sleep like a baby.

GINA

Well, you're out on a clear night anyhow.

KLEINMAN

Yes.

GINA

You can see a lot of stars.

KLEINMAN

Actually, I'm very nervous. I'd prefer to be home in bed. It's
weird at night. All the stores are closed. There's no traffic.
You can jaywalk . . . No one stops you . . .

GINA

Well, that's good, isn't it?

KLEINMAN

Er—it's a funny feeling. There's no civilization . . . I could
take my pants off and run naked down the main street.

GINA

Uh-huh.

KLEINMAN

I mean, I wouldn't. But I could.

GINA

To me the city at night is so cold and dark and empty. This must be what it's like in outer space.

KLEINMAN

I never cared for outer space.

GINA

But you're in outer space. We're just this big, round ball floating in space . . . You can't tell which way is up.

KLEINMAN

You think that's good? I'm a man who likes to know which way is up and which way is down and where's the bathroom.

GINA

You think there's life on any of those billions of stars out there?

KLEINMAN

I personally don't know. Although I hear there may be life on Mars, but the guy that told me is only in the hosiery business.

GINA

And it all goes on forever.

KLEINMAN

How can it go on forever? Sooner or later it must stop. Right? I mean sooner or later it must end and there's, er—a wall or something—be logical.

GINA

Are you saying the universe is finite?

KLEINMAN

I'm not saying anything. I don't want to get involved. I want to know what I'm supposed to be doing.

GINA

(Pointing it out)

There, you can see Gemini . . . the twins . . . and Orion
the hunter . . .

KLEINMAN

Where do you see twins? They hardly look alike.

GINA

Look at that tiny star out there . . . all alone. You can
barely see it.

KLEINMAN

You know how far that must be? I'd hate to tell you.

GINA

We're seeing the light that left that star millions of years
ago. It's just now reaching us.

KLEINMAN

I know what you mean.

GINA

Did you know that light travels 186,000 miles per second?

KLEINMAN

That's too fast if you ask me. I like to enjoy a thing. There's
no leisure any more.

GINA

For all we know that star disappeared millions of years ago
and it's taken that light, traveling 186,000 miles a second,
millions of years to reach us.

KLEINMAN

You're saying that star may not still be out there?

GINA

That's right.

KLEINMAN

Even though I see it with my own eyes?

GINA

That's right.

KLEINMAN

That's very scary, because if I see something with my own eyes, I like to think it's there. I mean, if that's true, they could all be like that—all burnt out—but we're just late getting the news.

GINA

Kleinman, who knows what's real?

KLEINMAN

What's real is what you can touch with your hands.

GINA

Oh? *(He kisses her; she responds passionately)* That'll be six dollars, please.

KLEINMAN

For what?

GINA

You had a little fun, didn't you?

KLEINMAN

A little, yes . . .

GINA

Well, I'm in business.

KLEINMAN

Yeah, but six dollars for a little kissing. For six dollars I could buy a muffler.

GINA

All right, give me five dollars.

KLEINMAN

Don't you ever kiss for nothing?

GINA

Kleinman, this is business. For pleasure, I kiss women.

KLEINMAN

Women? What a coincidence . . . me too.

GINA

I've got to go.

KLEINMAN

I didn't mean to insult you—

GINA

You didn't. I have to go.

KLEINMAN

Will you be okay?

GINA

I have my assignment to carry out. Good luck. I hope you find what you're supposed to do.

KLEINMAN
(Calling after her)
I didn't mean to act like an animal—I'm really one of the nicest people I know! *(And he's alone as her footsteps die out)* Well, this has gone far enough. I'm going home and that's it. Except then tomorrow they'll come around and ask where I was. They'll say, the plan went wrong, Kleinman, and it's your fault. How is it my fault? What's the difference. They'll find a way. They'll need a scapegoat. That's probably my part of the plan. I'm always blamed when nothing works. I—*(He hears a moan)* What? Who's that!?

DOCTOR
(Crawls onto the stage, mortally wounded)
Kleinman—

KLEINMAN

Doctor!

DOCTOR

I'm dying.

KLEINMAN

I'll get a doctor . . .

DOCTOR

I am a doctor.

KLEINMAN

Yes, but you're a dying doctor.

DOCTOR

It's too late—he caught me . . . ugh . . . There was no place to run.

KLEINMAN

Help! Help! Somebody come quickly!

DOCTOR

Don't yell, Kleinman . . . You don't want the killer to find you.

KLEINMAN

Listen, I don't care any more! Help! *(Then, thinking he might be found by the killer, he softens his voice)* Help . . . Who is he? Did you get a good look at him?

DOCTOR

No, just suddenly, a stab in the back.

KLEINMAN

Too bad, he didn't stab you from the front. You might have seen him.

DOCTOR

I'm dying, Kleinman—

KLEINMAN

It's nothing personal.

DOCTOR

What kind of stupid thing is that to say.

KLEINMAN

What can I say? I'm just trying to make conversation—
(A MAN runs on)

MAN

What's happening? Did someone call for help?

KLEINMAN

The doctor's dying . . . Get help . . . Wait! Did you hear
anything about me?

MAN

Who are you?

KLEINMAN

Kleinman.

MAN

Kleinman . . . Kleinman . . . Something, yes . . . They're
looking for you . . . It's important . . .

KLEINMAN

Who is?

MAN

Something to do with your assignment.

KLEINMAN

Finally.

MAN

I'll tell them I saw you.
(Runs off)

DOCTOR

Kleinman, do you believe in reincarnation?

KLEINMAN

What's that?

DOCTOR

Reincarnation—that a person comes back to life again as
something else.

KLEINMAN
Like what?

DOCTOR
Er . . . uh . . . another living thing . . .

KLEINMAN
What do you mean? Like an animal?

DOCTOR
Yes.

KLEINMAN
You mean like you may live again as a frog?

DOCTOR
Forget it, Kleinman, I didn't say anything.

KLEINMAN
Listen, anything's possible, but it's hard to imagine if a man
is president of a big corporation in this life, that he'll wind
up a chipmunk.

DOCTOR
It's getting black.

KLEINMAN
Look, why don't you tell me what your part in the plan is?
Since you'll be out of commission, I could take it over,
because so far I haven't been able to find out my
assignment.

DOCTOR
My assignment wouldn't do you any good. I'm the only one
who could carry it out.

KLEINMAN
For God's sake, I can't tell if we're too well organized or not
organized enough.

DOCTOR

Don't fail us, Kleinman. We need you.

(He dies)

KLEINMAN

Doctor? Doctor? Oh, my God . . . What do I do? The hell
with it. I'm going home! Let 'em all run around all night
like crackpots. The height of the season. No one'll tell me
anything. I just don't want them to blame me for everything. Well, why should they blame me? I came when they
called. They had nothing for me to do.

(A COP enters with the MAN who went looking for help)

MAN

Is there a dying man here?

KLEINMAN

I'm dying.

COP

You? What about him?

KLEINMAN

He's already dead.

COP

Were you a friend of his?

KLEINMAN

He took my tonsils out.

(COP kneels to inspect the body)

MAN

I was dead once.

KLEINMAN

Pardon me?

MAN

Dead: I've been dead. During the war. Wounded. There I
lay on an operating table. Surgeons sweating to save my

life. Suddenly they lost me—pulse stopped. It was all over. One of 'em, I'm told, had the presence of mind to massage my heart. Then it began beating again, so I lived, but for a tiny moment there, I was officially dead . . . According to science, too—dead . . . but that was a long time ago. That's why I can sympathize when I see one of these fellows.

KLEINMAN

So how was it?

MAN

What?

KLEINMAN

Being dead. Did you see anything?

MAN

No. It was just . . . nothing.

KLEINMAN

You don't remember any afterlife?

MAN

No.

KLEINMAN

My name didn't come up?

MAN

There was nothing. There is nothing after, Kleinman. Nothing.

KLEINMAN

I don't want to go. Not yet. Not now. I don't want what happened to him to happen to me. Trapped in an alley . . . stabbed . . . the others strangled . . . even Hacker . . . by this fiend.

MAN

Hacker wasn't murdered by the maniac.

KLEINMAN

No?

MAN

Hacker was assassinated by plotters.

KLEINMAN

Plotters?

MAN

The other faction.

KLEINMAN

What other faction?

MAN

You know about the other faction, don't you?

KLEINMAN

I don't know anything! I'm lost in the night.

MAN

Certain ones. Shepherd and Willis. They've always been at odds with Hacker's approach to the problem.

KLEINMAN

What?

MAN

Well, Hacker hasn't exactly gotten results.

KLEINMAN

Well, neither have the police.

POLICEMAN
(Rising)

We will, though. If the goddamn civilians would keep out of it.

KLEINMAN

I thought you wanted help.

POLICEMAN

Help, yes. Not a lot of confusion and panic. But don't worry. We've got a couple of clues and we're running data through our computers. These babies are the best electronic brains. Incapable of error. Let's see how long he holds out against them.

(Kneels)

KLEINMAN

So who killed Hacker?

POLICEMAN

There's a faction that opposes Hacker.

KLEINMAN

Who? Shepherd and Willis?

POLICEMAN

Plenty have defected to their side. Believe me. I even heard a group has splintered off from the new group.

KLEINMAN

Another faction?

POLICEMAN

With some pretty bright ideas on how to trap this fiend. It's what we need, isn't it? Different ideas? If one plan fails to achieve results, others crop up. That's natural. Or are you opposed to new ideas?

KLEINMAN

Me? No . . . but they killed Hacker . . .

MAN

Because he wouldn't let go. Because of his dogged insistence that his stupid scheme was the only one. Despite the fact that nothing was happening.

KLEINMAN

So now there are several plans? Or what?

MAN

Right. And I hope you're not married to Hacker's plan. Although plenty still are.

KLEINMAN

I don't even know Hacker's plan.

MAN

Good. Then maybe you can be useful to us.

KLEINMAN

Who's us?

MAN

Don't play innocent.

KLEINMAN

Who's playing?

MAN

Come on.

KLEINMAN

No, I don't know what's going on.

MAN
(Pulls knife on KLEINMAN)
Lives are at stake, you stupid vermin, make your choice.

KLEINMAN

Er . . . officer . . . Constable . . .

POLICEMAN

Now you want help, but last week we were fools because we couldn't catch the killer.

KLEINMAN

No criticism from me.

MAN

Choose, you worm.

POLICEMAN

Nobody gives a damn that we're working around the clock. Snowed under with crackpot confessions. One lunatic after another claiming to be the killer and begging for punishment.

MAN

I've got a good mind to cut your throat, the way you shilly-shally.

KLEINMAN

I'm ready to pitch in. Just tell me what I'm supposed to do.

MAN

Are you with Hacker or with us?

KLEINMAN

Hacker's dead.

MAN

He's got followers. Or maybe you'd rather go along with some splinter group. Eh?

KLEINMAN

If someone would just explain to me what each group stands for. You know what I mean? I never knew Hacker's plan . . . I don't know your plan. I don't know from splinter groups.

MAN

Isn't he the ignorant one, Jack?

POLICEMAN

Yeah. Knows it all until it's time to act. You make me sick. (*The remnants of HACKER'S GROUP enter*)

HANK

There you are, Kleinman. Where the hell have you been?

KLEINMAN

Me? Where've you been?

SAM

You wandered off just when we needed you.

KLEINMAN

No one said a word.

MAN

Kleinman's with *us* now.

JOHN

Is that true, Kleinman?

KLEINMAN

Is what true? I don't know what's true any more.
(Several MEN enter. They are an opposing group)

BILL

Hey, Frank. These guys giving you trouble?

FRANK

No. They couldn't if they wanted to.

AL

No?

FRANK

No.

AL

We could have had him trapped already if you boys were
where you should have been.

FRANK

We didn't agree with Hacker. His plan wasn't working.

DON

Yeah. We'll catch this killer. Leave it to us.

JOHN

We're not leaving anything to you. Let's go, Kleinman.

FRANK

You're not sticking with them, are you?

KLEINMAN

Me? I'm neutral. Whoever has the best plan.

HENRY

There are no neutrals, Kleinman.

MAN

It's us or them.

KLEINMAN

How can I choose when I don't know the alternatives? Is one apples? Is one pears? Are they both tangerines?

FRANK

Let's kill him now.

SAM

You're not doing any more killing.

FRANK

No?

SAM

No. And when we catch this maniac, someone's going to have to pay for Hacker.

KLEINMAN

While we're standing, arguing, the maniac could be killing someone. The object is to cooperate.

SAM

Tell that to them.

FRANK

Results is the name of the game.

DON

Let's take care of these bastards now. Otherwise they'll stand in our way and confuse the issues.

AL

Just try, big shot.

BILL

We'll do more than try.
(Knives and clubs pulled out and brandished)

KLEINMAN

Fellas—boys—

FRANK

Choose now, Kleinman, the moment is here!

HENRY

Better choose right, Kleinman. There's only going to be one winner.

KLEINMAN

We'll kill each other and the maniac'll remain loose. Don't you see? . . . They don't see.
(Fight starts. Suddenly everyone stops and looks up. Winding on stage is an impressive, religious-looking procession that enters, the ASSIST-ANT leading the way)

ASSISTANT

The murderer! We have located the maniac!
(Fight stops, buzzing, "What's this?" Noise: bong, bong. A group enters with HANS SPIRO, smelling and sniffing)

POLICEMAN

It's Spiro, the telepathic. We've brought him in on the case. He's clairvoyant.

KLEINMAN

Really? He must do well at the race track.

POLICEMAN

He's solved murders for others. All he needs is something to sniff or feel. He read my mind down at headquarters. Knew who I'd just been to bed with.

KLEINMAN

Your wife.

POLICEMAN
(After a dirty look at KLEINMAN)
Look at him, boys. Born with uncanny powers.

ASSISTANT
Mr. Spiro the clairvoyant is on the verge of revealing the
killer. Please clear the way. *(SPIRO, working his way, sniffing)*
Mr. Spiro wishes to sniff you.

KLEINMAN
Me?

ASSISTANT
Yes.

KLEINMAN
What for?

ASSISTANT
It's enough he wishes it.

KLEINMAN
I don't want to be sniffed.

FRANK
What have you got to hide?
(OTHERS ad-lib agreement)

KLEINMAN
Nothing, but it makes me nervous.

POLICEMAN
Go ahead. Sniff away.
(SPIRO sniffs. KLEINMAN is uncomfortable)

KLEINMAN
What is he doing? I got nothing to hide. My jacket
probably smells a little from camphor. Right? Hey, can you
stop sniffing me now? It makes me nervous.

AL
Nervous, Kleinman?

KLEINMAN

I never liked getting sniffed. *(SPIRO increases his intensity)*
What's the matter? What are you all looking at? What?
Oh, I know. I spilled some salad dressing on my pants . . .
So there's a faint odor—not too terrible . . . It was the
house dressing over at Wilton's Steak House . . . I like
steak . . . not rare . . . Well, yes, rare, I mean not raw
. . . You know, you order rare and it comes all red?

SPIRO

This man is a murderer.

KLEINMAN

What?

POLICEMAN

Kleinman?

SPIRO

Yes. Kleinman.

POLICEMAN

No!

ASSISTANT

Mr. Spiro has done it again!

KLEINMAN

What are you talking about? Do you know what you're
talking about?

SPIRO

Here is the guilty party.

KLEINMAN

You're crazy. Spiro . . . this guy's a lunatic!

HENRY

So, Kleinman, it's been you all along.

FRANK
(Yelling)
Hey—here! Here! We've trapped him!

KLEINMAN
What are you doing?!

SPIRO
There is no doubt. It's conclusive.

BILL
Why'd you do it, Kleinman?

KLEINMAN
Do what? You're going to believe this guy? From smelling
me?

ASSISTANT
Mr. Spiro's uncanny power has never failed him yet.

KLEINMAN
This guy's a fake. What's with the smelling!?

SAM
So Kleinman's the murderer.

KLEINMAN
No . . . fellas . . . you all know me!

JOHN
Why'd you do it, Kleinman?

FRANK
Yeah.

AL
He did it because he's crazy. Loco in the head.

KLEINMAN
I'm crazy? Look at the way I'm dressed!

HENRY
Don't expect him to make sense. His mind's gone.

BILL

That's how it is with a crazy man. They can be logical on every point except one—their weakness, their point of insanity.

SAM

And Kleinman's always so damn logical.

HENRY

Too damn logical.

KLEINMAN

This is a joke, right? Because if it's not a joke I'm going to start to cry.

SPIRO

Once again I thank the Lord for the special gift He has seen fit to bestow on me.

JOHN

Let's string him up right now!
(General agreement)

KLEINMAN

Don't come near me! I don't like string!

GINA
(The prostitute)

He tried to attack me! He grabbed me suddenly!

KLEINMAN

I gave you six dollars!
(They grab him)

BILL

I got some rope!

KLEINMAN

What are you doing?

FRANK

We'll make this city safe once and for all.

KLEINMAN
You're hanging the wrong man. I wouldn't hurt a fly . . .
okay, a fly maybe—

POLICEMAN
We can't hang him without a trial.

KLEINMAN
Of course not. I have certain rights.

AL
What about the rights of the victims, eh?

KLEINMAN
What victims? I want my lawyer! You hear! I want my
lawyer! I don't even have a lawyer!

POLICEMAN
How do you plead, Kleinman?

KLEINMAN
Not guilty. Completely not guilty! I'm not now nor have I
ever been a homicidal killer. It doesn't interest me even as a
hobby.

HENRY
What have you done to contribute to the capture of the
killer?

KLEINMAN
You mean the plan? Nobody told me what it is.

JOHN
Don't you think it's your responsibility to find out for
yourself?

KLEINMAN
How? Every time I asked I got a song and dance.

AL
It's your responsibility, Kleinman.

FRANK

That's right. It's not as if there was only one plan.

BILL

Sure. We came up with an alternate plan.

DON

And there were other plans. You could have gotten in on something.

SAM

Is that why you were having trouble choosing? Because you didn't want to choose?

KLEINMAN

Choose between what? Tell me the plan. Let me help. Use me.

POLICEMAN

It's a little late for that.

HENRY

Kleinman, you have been judged and found guilty. You will hang. Do you have any final requests?

KLEINMAN

Yes. I'd prefer not to hang.

HENRY

I'm sorry, Kleinman. There's nothing we can do.

ABE

(Enters in a tizzy)

Quickly—come quickly!

JOHN

What is it?

ABE

We've got the murderer trapped behind the warehouse.

AL

That's impossible. Kleinman's the killer.

ABE

No. He was discovered in the act of strangling Edith Cox. She identified him. Hurry. We need everyone we can get.

SAM

Is it anyone we know?

ABE

No. It's a stranger, but he's on the run!

KLEINMAN

See! See! You were all ready to hang an innocent man.

HENRY

Forgive us, Kleinman.

KLEINMAN

Sure. Anytime you run out of ideas, just drop over with a rope.

SPIRO

There must be some mistake.

KLEINMAN

And you? You ought to have a nose job! *(They all run off)* It's good to know who your friends are. I'm going home! This is no longer my problem! . . . I'm tired, I'm cold . . . some night . . . Now, where am I? . . . Boy, my sense of direction I wouldn't give you two cents for . . . No, that's not right . . . I got to rest a second—get my bearings . . . I'm a little sick from fear . . . *(A noise)* Oh, God . . . now what?

MANIAC

Kleinman?

KLEINMAN

Who are you?

MANIAC
(Who resembles KLEINMAN)
The homicidal killer. Can I sit down? I'm exhausted.

KLEINMAN
What?

MANIAC
Everybody's chasing me . . . I'm running up alleys and in and out of doorways. I'm slinking around town—and they think I'm having fun.

KLEINMAN
You're—the killer?

MANIAC
Sure.

KLEINMAN
I've got to get out of here!

MANIAC
Don't get excited. I'm armed.

KLEINMAN
You—you're going to kill me?

MANIAC
Of course. That's my specialty.

KLEINMAN
You—you're crazy.

MANIAC
Sure I'm crazy. You think a sane person would go around killing people? And I don't even rob them. It's the truth. I never made a penny on a single victim. I never took a pocket comb.

KLEINMAN
So why do you do it?

MANIAC

Why? Because I'm crazy.

KLEINMAN

But you look okay.

MANIAC

You can't go by physical appearance. I'm a maniac.

KLEINMAN

Yeah, but I expected a tall, black, frightening figure . . .

MANIAC

This is not the movies, Kleinman. I'm a man like you.
What should I have, fangs?

KLEINMAN

But you've killed so many big, powerful men . . . twice
your size . . .

MANIAC

Sure. Because I come up from behind or I wait till they're
asleep. Listen, I'm not looking for trouble.

KLEINMAN

But why do you do it?

MANIAC

I'm a screwball. You think I know?

KLEINMAN

Do you like it?

MANIAC

It's not a question of *like*. I do it.

KLEINMAN

But don't you see how ridiculous it is?

MANIAC

If I could see that, I'd be sane.

KLEINMAN

How long have you been this way?

MANIAC

As far as I can remember.

KLEINMAN

Can't you be helped?

MANIAC

By who?

KLEINMAN

There's doctors . . . clinics . . .

MANIAC

You think doctors know anything? I been to doctors. I've had blood tests, x-rays. They don't find the craziness. That doesn't show up on an x-ray.

KLEINMAN

What about psychiatry? Mental doctors?

MANIAC

I fool them.

KLEINMAN

Huh?

MANIAC

I act normal. They show me ink blots . . . They ask me if I like girls. I tell 'em sure.

KLEINMAN

This is terrible.

MANIAC

You got any last wishes?

KLEINMAN

You can't be serious!

MANIAC

You wanna hear my crazy laugh?

KLEINMAN

No. Can't you listen to reason? *(MANIAC snaps the switch-blade open dramatically)* If you don't get any thrill out of killing me, why do it? It's not logical. You could be using your time constructively . . . Take up golf—be a crazy golfer!

MANIAC

Goodbye, Kleinman!

KLEINMAN

Help! Help! Murder! *(And he's stabbed. The MANIAC runs off)* Ohhh! Ohh!
(A small crowd gathers. We hear: He's dying. KLEINMAN's dying . . . he's dying . . .)

JOHN

Kleinman . . . what was he like?

KLEINMAN

Like me.

JOHN

What do you mean, like you?

KLEINMAN

He looked like me.

JOHN

But Jensen said he looked like Jensen . . . tall and blond, Swedish-looking . . .

KLEINMAN

Oooh . . . You gonna listen to Jensen or you gonna listen to me?

JOHN

All right, don't get angry . . .

KLEINMAN

All right, then don't talk like a jerk . . . He looked like
me . . .

JOHN

Unless he's a master of disguise . . .

KLEINMAN

Well, he's sure a master of something, and you guys better
get on the ball.

JOHN

Bring him some water.

KLEINMAN

What do I need water for?

JOHN

I assumed you were thirsty.

KLEINMAN

Dying doesn't make you thirsty. Unless you get stabbed
after eating herring.

JOHN

Are you afraid to die?

KLEINMAN

It's not that I'm afraid to die, I just don't want to be there
when it happens.

JOHN
(Musing)

Sooner or later he'll get all of us.

KLEINMAN
(Delirious)

Cooperate . . . God is the only enemy.

JOHN

Poor Kleinman. He's delirious.

KLEINMAN

Oh . . . oh . . . ugggmmmfff.

(Dies)

JOHN

Come on, we've got to come up with a better plan.

(They start going off)

KLEINMAN

(Rises a bare bit)

And another thing. If there is a life after death and we all wind up in the same place—don't call me, I'll call you.

(Expires)

MAN

(Runs on)

The killer's been spotted by the railroad tracks! Come quickly!

(They all go off in pursuit and we
                BLACKOUT)

The Early Essays

Following are a few of the early essays of Woody Allen. There are no late essays, because he ran out of observations. Perhaps as Allen grows older he will understand more of life and will set it down, and then retire to his bedroom and remain there indefinitely. Like the essays of Bacon, Allen's are brief and full of practical wisdom, although space does not permit the inclusion of his most profound statement, "Looking at the Bright Side."

ON SEEING A TREE IN SUMMER

Of all the wonders of nature, a tree in summer is perhaps the most remarkable, with the possible exception of a moose singing "Embraceable You" in spats. Consider the leaves, so green and leafy (if not, something is wrong). Behold how the branches reach up to heaven as if to say, "Though I am only a branch, still I would love to collect Social Security." And the varieties! Is this tree a spruce or poplar? Or a giant redwood? No, I'm afraid it's a stately elm, and once again you've made an ass of yourself. Of course, you'd know all the trees in a minute if you were nature's creature the woodpecker, but then it would be too late and you'd never get your car started.

But why is a tree so much more delightful than, say, a babbling brook? Or anything that babbles, for that matter? Because its glorious presence is mute testimony to an intelligence far greater than any on earth, certainly in the present Administration. As the poet said, "Only God can make a tree"—probably because it's so hard to figure out how to get the bark on.

Once a lumberjack was about to chop down a tree, when he noticed a heart carved on it, with two names inside. Putting away his axe, he sawed down the tree instead. The point of that story escapes me, although six months later the lumberjack was fined for teaching a dwarf Roman numerals.

ON YOUTH AND AGE

. . . .

The true test of maturity is not how old a person is but how he reacts to awakening in the midtown area in his shorts. What do years matter, particularly if your apartment is rent-controlled? The thing to remember is that each time of life has its appropriate rewards, whereas when you're dead it's hard to find the light switch. The chief problem about death, incidentally, is the fear that there may be no afterlife—a depressing thought, particularly for those who have bothered to shave. Also, there is the fear that there is an afterlife but no one will know where it's being held. On the plus side, death is one of the few things that can be done as easily lying down.

Consider, then: Is old age really so terrible? Not if you've brushed your teeth faithfully! And why is there no buffer to the onslaught of the years? Or a good hotel in downtown Indianapolis? Oh, well.

In short, the best thing to do is behave in a manner befitting one's age. If you are sixteen or under, try not to go bald. On the other hand, if you are over eighty, it is extremely good form to shuffle down the street clutching a brown paper bag and muttering, "The Kaiser will steal my string." Remember, everything is relative—or should be. If it's not, we must begin again.

On Frugality

· · · · · · · · ·

As one goes through life, it is extremely important to conserve funds, and one should never spend money on anything foolish, like pear nectar or a solid-gold hat. Money is not everything, but it is better than having one's health. After all, one cannot go into a butcher shop and tell the butcher, "Look at my great suntan, and besides I never catch colds," and expect him to hand over any merchandise. (Unless, of course, the butcher is an idiot.) Money is better than poverty, if only for financial reasons. Not that it can buy happiness. Take the case of the ant and the grasshopper: The grasshopper played all summer, while the ant worked and saved. When winter came, the grasshopper had nothing, but the ant complained of chest pains. Life is hard for insects. And don't think mice are having any fun, either. The point is, we all need a nest egg to fall back on, but not while wearing a good suit.

Finally, let us bear in mind that it is easier to spend two dollars than to save one. And for God's sake don't invest money with any brokerage firm in which one of the partners is named Frenchy.

On Love

· · · · · · · ·

Is it better to be the lover or the loved one? Neither, if your cholesterol is over six hundred. By love, of course, I refer to romantic love—the love between man and woman, rather than between mother and child, or a boy and his dog, or two headwaiters.

The marvelous thing is that when one is in love there is an impulse to sing. This must be resisted at all costs, and care must also be taken to see that the ardent male doesn't "talk" the lyrics of songs. To be loved, certainly, is different from being admired, as one can be admired from afar but to really love someone it is essential to be in the same room with the person, crouching behind the drapes.

To be a really good lover, then, one must be strong and yet tender. How strong? I suppose being able to lift fifty pounds should do it. Bear in mind also that to the lover the loved one is always the most beautiful thing imaginable, even though to a stranger she may be indistinguishable from an order of smelts. Beauty is in the eye of the beholder. Should the beholder have poor eyesight, he can ask the nearest person which girls look good. (Actually, the prettiest ones are almost always the most boring, and that is why some people feel there is no God.)

"The joys of love are but a moment long," sang the troubadour, "but the pain of love endures forever." This was almost a hit song, but the melody was too close to "I'm a Yankee Doodle Dandy."

On Tripping Through a Copse and Picking Violets

. . . .

This is no fun at all, and I would recommend almost any other activity. Try visiting a sick friend. If this is impossible, see a show or get into a nice warm tub and read. Anything is better than turning up in a copse with one of those vacuous smiles and accumulating flowers in a basket. Next thing you know, you'll be skipping to and fro. What are you going to do with the violets once you get them, anyhow? "Why, put them in a vase," you say. What a stupid answer. Nowadays you call the florist and order by phone. Let *him* trip through the copse, he's getting paid for it. That way, if an electrical storm comes up or a beehive is chanced upon, it will be the florist who is rushed to Mount Sinai.

Do not conclude from this, incidentally, that I am

insensitive to the joys of nature, although I have come to the conclusion that for sheer fun it is hard to beat forty-eight hours at Foam Rubber City during the high holidays. But that is another story.

A Brief, Yet Helpful, Guide to Civil Disobedience

In perpetrating a revolution, there are two requirements: someone or something to revolt against and someone to actually show up and do the revolting. Dress is usually casual and both parties may be flexible about time and place but if either faction fails to attend, the whole enterprise is likely to come off badly. In the Chinese Revolution of 1650 neither party showed up and the deposit on the hall was forfeited.

The people or parties revolted against are called the "oppressors" and are easily recognized as they seem to be the ones having all the fun. The "oppressors" generally get to wear suits, own land, and play their radios late at night without being yelled at. Their job is to maintain the "status quo," a condition where everything remains the same although they may be willing to paint every two years.

When the "oppressors" become too strict, we have what is known as a police state, wherein all dissent is forbidden, as is chuckling, showing up in a bow tie, or referring to the mayor as "Fats." Civil liberties are greatly curtailed in a police state, and freedom of speech is unheard of, although one is allowed to mime to a record. Opinions critical of the government are not tolerated, particularly about their dancing. Freedom of the press is also curtailed and the ruling party "manages" the news, permitting the citizens to hear only acceptable political ideas and ball scores that will not cause unrest.

The groups who revolt are called the "oppressed" and can generally be seen milling about and grumbling or claiming to have headaches. (It should be noted that the oppressors never revolt and attempt to become the oppressed as that would entail a change of underwear.)

Some famous examples of revolutions are:

The French Revolution, in which the peasants seized power by force and quickly changed all locks on the palace doors so the nobles could not get back in. Then they had a large party and gorged themselves. When the nobles finally recaptured the palace they were forced to clean up and found many stains and cigarette burns.

The Russian Revolution, which simmered for years and suddenly erupted when the serfs finally realized that the Czar and the Tsar were the same person.

It should be noted that after a revolution is over, the "oppressed" frequently take over and begin acting like the "oppressors." Of course by then it is very hard to get them on the phone and money lent for cigarettes and gum during the fighting may as well be forgotten about.

Methods of Civil disobedience:

Hunger Strike. Here the oppressed goes without food until his demands are met. Insidious politicians will often leave biscuits within easy reach or perhaps some cheddar cheese, but they must be resisted. If the party in power can get the striker to eat, they usually have little trouble putting down the insurrection. If they can get him to eat and also lift the check, they have won for sure. In Pakistan, a hunger strike was broken when the government produced an exceptionally fine veal cordon bleu which the masses found was too appealing to turn down, but such gourmet dishes are rare.

The problem with the hunger strike is that after several days one can get quite hungry, particularly since sound trucks are paid to go through the street saying, "Um . . . what nice chicken—umm . . . some peas . . . umm . . ."

A modified form of the Hunger Strike for those whose political convictions are not quite so radical is giving up chives. This small gesture, when used properly, can greatly influence a government, and it is well known that Mahatma Gandhi's insistence on eating his salads untossed shamed the British government into many concessions. Other things besides food one can give up are: whist, smiling, and standing on one foot and imitating a crane.

Sit-down Strike. Proceed to a designated spot and then sit down, but sit all the way down. Otherwise you are squatting, a position that makes no political point unless the government is also squatting. (This is rare, although a government will occasionally crouch in cold weather.) The trick is to remain seated until concessions are made, but as in the Hunger Strike, the government will try subtle means of making the striker rise. They may say, "Okay, everybody up, we're closing." Or, "Can you get up for a minute, we'd just like to see how tall you are?"

Demonstration and Marches. The key point about a demonstration is that it must be seen. Hence the term "demonstration." If a person demonstrates privately in his own home, this is not technically a demonstration but merely "acting silly" or "behaving like an ass."

A fine example of a demonstration was the Boston Tea Party, where outraged Americans disguised as Indians dumped British tea into the harbor. Later, Indians disguised as outraged Americans dumped actual British into the harbor. Following that, the British disguised as tea, dumped each other into the harbor. Finally, German mercenaries clad only in costumes from *The Trojan Women* leapt into the harbor for no apparent reason.

When demonstrating, it is good to carry a placard stating

one's position. Some suggested positions are: (1) lower taxes, (2) raise taxes, and (3) stop grinning at Persians.

Miscellaneous methods of Civil Disobedience:

Standing in front of City Hall and chanting the word "pudding" until one's demands are met.

Tying up traffic by leading a flock of sheep into the shopping area.

Phoning members of "the establishment" and singing "Bess, You Is My Woman Now" into the phone.

Dressing as a policeman and then skipping.

Pretending to be an artichoke but punching people as they pass.

Match Wits with Inspector Ford

THE CASE OF THE MURDERED SOCIALITE
. . . .

Inspector Ford burst into the study. On the floor was the body of Clifford Wheel, who apparently had been struck from behind with a croquet mallet. The position of the body indicated that the victim had been surprised in the act of singing "Sorrento" to his goldfish. Evidence showed there had been a terrible struggle that had twice been interrupted by phone calls, one a wrong number and one asking if the victim was interested in dance lessons.

Before Wheel had died, he had dipped his finger into the inkwell and scrawled out a message: "Fall Sale Prices Drastically Reduced—Everything Must Go!"

"A businessman to the end," mused Ives, his manservant, whose elevator shoes, curiously enough, made him two inches shorter.

The door to the terrace was open and footprints led from there, down the hall and into a drawer.

"Where were you when it happened, Ives?"

"In the kitchen. Doing the dishes." Ives produced some suds from his wallet to corroborate his story.

"Did you hear anything?"

"He was in there with some men. They were arguing over who was tallest. I thought I heard Mr. Wheel start yodeling and Mosley, his business partner, began yelling, 'My God, I'm going bald!' Next thing I knew, there was a harp glissando and Mr. Wheel's head came rolling out onto the lawn. I heard Mr. Mosley threaten him. He said if Mr. Wheel touched his grapefruit again, he would not cosign a bank loan for him. I think he killed him."

"Does the terrace door open from the inside or from the outside?" Inspector Ford asked Ives.

"From the outside. Why?"

"Exactly as I suspected. I now realize it was you, not Mosley, who killed Clifford Wheel."

How Did Inspector Ford Know?

Because of the layout of the house, Ives could not have sneaked up behind his employer. He would have had to sneak up in front of him, at which time Mr. Wheel would have stopped singing "Sorrento" and used the mallet on Ives, a ritual they had gone through many times.

A Curious Riddle
. . . .

Apparently, Walker was a suicide. Overdose of sleeping pills. Still, something seemed amiss to Inspector Ford. Perhaps it was the position of the body. Inside the TV set, looking out. On the floor was a cryptic suicide note. "Dear Edna, My woolen suit itches me, and so I have decided to take my own life. See that our son finishes all his push-ups. I leave you my entire fortune, with the exception of my porkpie hat, which I hereby donate to the planetarium. Please don't feel sorry for me, as I enjoy being dead and much prefer it to paying rent. Goodbye, Henry. P.S. This may not be the time to bring it up, but I have every reason to believe that your brother is dating a Cornish hen."

Edna Walker bit her lower lip nervously. "What do you make of it, Inspector?"

Inspector Ford looked at the bottle of sleeping pills on the night table. "How long had your husband been an insomniac?"

"For years. It was psychological. He was afraid that if he closed his eyes, the city would paint a white line down him."

"I see. Did he have any enemies?"

"Not really. Except for some gypsies who ran a tearoom on the outskirts of town. He insulted them once by putting on a pair of earmuffs and hopping up and down in place on their sabbath."

Inspector Ford noticed a half-finished glass of milk on the desk. It was still warm. "Mrs. Walker, is your son away at college?"

"I'm afraid not. He was expelled last week for immoral conduct. It came as quite a surprise. They caught him trying to immerse a dwarf in tartar sauce. That's one thing they won't tolerate at an Ivy League school."

"And one thing I won't tolerate is murder. Your son is under arrest."

Why Did Inspector Ford Suspect
Walker's Son Had Killed Him?

Mr. Walker's body was found with cash in his pockets. A man who was going to commit suicide would be sure to take a credit card and sign for everything.

THE STOLEN GEM
. . . .

The glass case was shattered and the Bellini Sapphire was missing. The only clues left behind at the museum were a blond hair and a dozen fingerprints, all pinkies. The guard explained that he had been standing there when a black-clad figure crept up behind him and struck him over the head with some notes for a speech. Just before losing consciousness, he thought he had heard a man's voice say, "Jerry, call your mother," but he could not be sure. Apparently, the thief had entered through the skylight and walked down the wall with suction shoes, like a human fly. The museum guards always kept an enormous fly swatter for just such occasions, but this time they had been fooled.

"Why would anyone want the Bellini Sapphire?" the museum curator asked. "Don't they know it's cursed?"

"What's this about a curse?" Inspector Ford was quick to ask.

"The sapphire was originally owned by a sultan who died under mysterious circumstances when a hand reached out of a bowl of soup he was eating and strangled him. The next owner was an English lord who was found one day by his wife growing upside down in a window box. Nothing was heard of the stone for a while; then it turned up years later in the possession of a Texas millionaire, who was brushing his teeth when he suddenly caught fire. We purchased the sapphire only last month, but the curse seemed to be working still, because shortly after we obtained it, the entire board of trustees at the museum formed a conga line and danced off a cliff."

"Well," Inspector Ford said, "it may be an unlucky jewel, but it's valuable, and if you want it back, go to Handleman's Delicatessen and arrest Leonard Handleman. You'll find that the sapphire is in his pocket."

How Did Inspector Ford Know
Who the Jewel Thief Was?

The previous day, Leonard Handleman had remarked, "Boy, if I only had a large sapphire, I could get out of the delicatessen business."

THE MACABRE ACCIDENT
· · · · · · · · · · · · ·

"I just shot my husband," wept Cynthia Freem as she stood over the body of the burly man in the snow.

"How did it happen?" asked Inspector Ford, getting right to the point.

"We were hunting. Quincy loved to hunt, as did I. We got separated momentarily. The bushes were overgrown. I guess I thought he was a woodchuck. I blasted away. It was too late. As I was removing his pelt, I realized we were married."

"Hmm," mused Inspector Ford, glancing at the foot-prints in the snow. "You must be a very good shot. You managed to plug him right between the eyebrows."

"Oh, no, it was lucky. I'm really quite an amateur at that sort of thing."

"I see." Inspector Ford examined the dead man's posses-sions. In his pocket there was some string, also an apple from 1904 and instructions on what to do if you wake up next to an Armenian.

"Mrs. Freem, was this your husband's first hunting accident?"

"His first fatal one, yes. Although once in the Canadian Rockies, an eagle carried off his birth certificate."

"Did your husband always wear a toupee?"

"Not really. He would usually carry it with him and produce it if challenged in an argument. Why?"

"He sounds eccentric."

"He was."

"Is that why you killed him?"

How Did Inspector Ford Know
It Was No Accident?

An experienced hunter like Quincy Freem would never

have stalked deer in his underwear. Actually, Mrs. Freem had bludgeoned him to death at home while he was playing the spoons and had tried to make it look like a hunting accident by dragging his body to the woods and leaving a copy of *Field & Stream* nearby. In her haste, she had forgotten to dress him. Why he had been playing the spoons in his underwear remains a mystery.

THE BIZARRE KIDNAPPING
. . . .

Half-starved, Kermit Kroll staggered into the living room of his parents' home, where they waited anxiously with Inspector Ford.

"Thanks for paying the ransom, folks," Kermit said. "I never thought I'd get out of there alive."

"Tell me about it," the inspector said.

"I was on my way downtown to have my hat blocked when a sedan pulled up and two men asked me if I wanted to see a horse that could recite the Gettysburg Address. I said sure and got in. Next thing, I'm chloroformed and wake up somewhere tied to a chair and blindfolded."

Inspector Ford examined the ransom note. "Dear Mom and Dad, Leave $50,000 in a bag under the bridge on Decatur Street. If there is no bridge on Decatur Street, please build one. I am being treated well, given shelter and good food, although last night the clams casino were overcooked. Send the money quickly, because if they don't hear from you within several days, the man who now makes up my bed will strangle me. Yours, Kermit. P.S. This is no joke. I am enclosing a joke so you will be able to tell the difference."

"Do you have any idea at all as to where you were being held?"

"No, I just kept hearing an odd noise outside the window."

"Odd?"

"Yes. You know the sound a herring makes when you lie to it?"

"Hmm," reflected Inspector Ford. "And how did you finally escape?"

"I told them I wanted to go to the football game but I only had a single ticket. They said okay, as long as I kept the blindfold on and promised to return by midnight. I complied, but during the third quarter, the Bears had a big lead, so I left and made my way back here."

"Very interesting," Inspector Ford said. "Now I know this kidnapping was a put-up job. I believe you're in on it and are splitting the money."

How Did Inspector Ford Know?

Although Kermit Kroll did still live with his parents, they were eighty and he was sixty. Actual kidnappers would never abduct a sixty-year-old child, as it makes no sense.

The Irish
Genius

Viscous and Sons has announced publication of *The Annotated Poems of Sean O'Shawn*, the great Irish poet, considered
by many to be the most incomprehensible and hence the
finest poet of his time. Abounding in highly personal
references, any understanding of O'Shawn's work requires
an intimate knowledge of his life, which, according to
scholars, not even he had.

Following is a sample from this fine book.

Beyond Ichor

Let us sail. Sail with
Fogarty's chin to Alexandria,
While the Beamish Brothers
Hurry giggling to the tower,
Proud of their gums.
A thousand years passed since
Agamemnon said, "Don't open
The gates, who the hell needs
A wooden horse that size?"
What is the connection? Only

That Shaunnesy, with dying
Breath, refused to order an
Appetizer with his meal although
He was entitled to it.
And brave Bixby, despite his
Resemblance to a woodpecker,
Could not retrieve his underwear
From Socrates without a ticket.

Parnell had the answer, but no
One would ask him the question.
No one but old Lafferty, whose
Lapis lazuli practical joke caused
A whole generation to take
Samba lessons.
True, Homer was blind and that
Accounted for why he dated those
Particular women.
But Aegnus and the Druids bear
Mute testimony to man's quest
For free alterations.
Blake dreamed of it too, and
O'Higgins who had his suit
Stolen while he was still in it.
Civilization is shaped like a
Circle and repeats itself, while
O'Leary's head is shaped like
A trapezoid.
Rejoice! Rejoice! And call your
Mother once in a while.

Let us sail. O'Shawn was fond of sailing, although he had
never done it on the sea. As a boy he dreamed of becoming
a ship's captain but gave it up when someone explained to
him what sharks were. His older brother James, however,
did go off and join the British Navy, though he was
dishonorably discharged for selling coleslaw to a bosun.

Fogarty's chin. Undoubtedly a reference to George Fogarty, who convinced O'Shawn to become a poet and assured him he would still be invited to parties. Fogarty published a magazine for new poets and although its circulation was limited to his mother, its impact was international.

Fogarty was a fun-loving, rubicund Irishman whose idea of a good time was to lie down in the public square and imitate a tweezers. Eventually he suffered a nervous breakdown and was arrested for eating a pair of pants on Good Friday.

Fogarty's chin was an object of great ridicule because it was tiny to the point of nonexistence, and at Jim Kelly's wake, he told O'Shawn, "I'd give anything for a larger chin. If I don't find one soon I'm liable to do something rash." Fogarty, incidentally, was a friend of Bernard Shaw's and was once permitted to touch Shaw's beard, provided he would go away.

Alexandria. References to the Middle East appear throughout O'Shawn's work, and his poem that begins "To Bethlehem with suds . . ." deals caustically with the hotel business seen through the eyes of a mummy.

The Beamish Brothers. Two half-wit brothers who tried to get from Belfast to Scotland by mailing each other.

Liam Beamish went to Jesuit school with O'Shawn but was thrown out for dressing like a beaver. Quincy Beamish was the more introverted of the two and kept a furniture pad on his head till he was forty-one.

The Beamish Brothers used to pick on O'Shawn and usually ate his lunch just before he did. Still, O'Shawn remembers them fondly and in his best sonnet, "My love is like a great, great yak," they appear symbolically as end tables.

The tower. When O'Shawn moved out of his parent's home, he lived in a tower just south of Dublin. It was a very low tower, standing about six feet, or two inches shorter than O'Shawn. He shared this residence with Harry

O'Connel, a friend with literary pretensions, whose verse play *The Musk Ox*, closed abruptly when the cast was chloroformed.

O'Connel was a great influence on O'Shawn's style and ultimately convinced him that every poem need not begin, "Roses are red, violets are blue."

Proud of their gums. The Beamish Brothers had unusually fine gums. Liam Beamish could remove his false teeth and eat peanut brittle, which he did every day for sixteen years until someone told him there was no such profession.

Agamemnon. O'Shawn was obsessed with the Trojan War. He could not believe an army could be so stupid as to accept a gift from its enemy during wartime. Particularly when they got close to the wooden horse and heard giggling inside. This episode seems to have traumatized the young O'Shawn and throughout his entire life he examined every gift given him very carefully, going so far as to shine a flashlight into a pair of shoes he received on his birthday and calling out, "Anybody in there? Eh? Come on out!"

Shaunnesy. Michael Shaunnesy, an occult writer and mystic, who convinced O'Shawn there would be a life after death for those who saved string.

Shaunnesy also believed the moon influenced actions and that to take a haircut during a total eclipse caused sterility. O'Shawn was very much taken with Shaunnesy and devoted much of his life to occult studies, although he never achieved his final goal of being able to enter a room through the keyhole.

The moon figures heavily in O'Shawn's later poems, and he told James Joyce that one of his greatest pleasures was to immerse his arm in custard on a moonlit night.

The reference to Shaunnesy's refusing an appetizer probably refers to the time the two men dined together in Innesfree and Shaunnesy blew chickpeas through a straw at a fat lady when she disagreed with his views on embalming.

Bixby. Eamon Bixby. A political fanatic who preached ventriloquism as a cure for the world's ills. He was a great student of Socrates but differed from the Greek philosopher in his idea of the "good life," which Bixby felt was impossible unless everybody weighed the same.

Parnell had the answer. The answer O'Shawn refers to is "Tin," and the question is "What is the chief export of Bolivia?" That no one asked Parnell the question is understandable, although he was challenged once to name the largest fur-bearing quadruped extant and he said, "Chicken," for which he was severely criticized.

Lafferty. John Millington Synge's podiatrist. A fascinating character who had a passionate affair with Molly Bloom until he realized she was a fictional character.

Lafferty was fond of practical jokes and once with some corn meal and egg, he breaded Synge's arch supports. Synge walked peculiarly as a result, and his followers imitated him, hoping that by duplicating his gait, they too would write fine plays. Hence the lines: "caused/A whole generation to take/Samba lessons."

Homer was blind. Homer was a symbol for T. S. Eliot, whom O'Shawn considered a poet of "immense scope but very little breadth."

The two men met in London at rehearsals of *Murder in the Cathedral* (at that time entitled *Million Dollar Legs*). O'Shawn persuaded Eliot to abandon his sideburns and give up any notion he might have of becoming a Spanish dancer. Both writers then composed a manifesto stating the aims of the "new poetry," one of which was to write fewer poems that dealt with rabbits.

Aegnus and the Druids. O'Shawn was influenced by Celtic mythology, and his poem that begins, "Clooth na bare, na bare, na bare . . ." tells how the gods of ancient Ireland transformed two lovers into a set of the Encyclopaedia Britannica.

Free alterations. Probably refers to O'Shawn's wish to "alter the human race," whom he felt were basically depraved, especially jockeys. O'Shawn was definitely a pessimist and felt that no good could come of mankind until they agreed to lower their body temperature from 98.6, which he felt was unreasonable.

Blake. O'Shawn was a mystic and, like Blake, believed in unseen forces. This was confirmed for him when his brother Ben was struck by lightning while licking a postage stamp. The lightning failed to kill Ben, which O'Shawn attributed to Providence, although it took his brother seventeen years before he could get his tongue back in his mouth.

O'Higgins. Patrick O'Higgins introduced O'Shawn to Polly Flaherty, who was to become O'Shawn's wife after a courtship of ten years in which the two did nothing more than meet secretly and wheeze at each other. Polly never realized the extent of her husband's genius and told intimates she thought he would be most remembered not for his poetry but for his habit of emitting a piercing shriek just before eating apples.

O'Leary's head. Mount O'Leary, where O'Shawn proposed to Polly just before she rolled off. O'Shawn visited her in the hospital and won her heart with his poem "On the Decomposing of Flesh."

Call your mother. On her deathbed, O'Shawn's mother, Bridget, begged her son to abandon poetry and become a vacuum-cleaner salesman. O'Shawn couldn't promise and suffered from anxiety and guilt the rest of his life, although at the International Poetry Conference in Geneva, he sold W. H. Auden and Wallace Stevens each a Hoover.

God

. . . .

A PLAY

scene: Athens. Approximately 500 b.c. Two distraught Greeks in the center of enormous empty amphitheater. Sunset. One is the ACTOR; the other, the WRITER. They are both thinking and distracted. They should be played by two good, broad burlesque clowns.

ACTOR

Nothing . . . just nothing . . .

WRITER

What?

ACTOR

Meaningless. It's empty.

WRITER

The ending.

ACTOR

Of course. What are we discussing? We're discussing the ending.

WRITER

We're always discussing the ending.

ACTOR

Because it's hopeless.

WRITER

I admit it's unsatisfying.

ACTOR

Unsatisfying!? It's not even believable. The trick is to start at the ending when you write a play. Get a good strong ending and then write backwards.

WRITER

I've tried that. I got a play with no beginning.

ACTOR

That's absurd.

WRITER

Absurd? What's absurd?

ACTOR

Every play must have a beginning, middle, and end.

WRITER

Why?

ACTOR
(Confidently)
Because everything in nature has a beginning, middle, and end.

WRITER

What about a circle?

ACTOR
(Thinks)
Okay . . . A circle has no beginning, middle, or end—but they're not much fun either.

WRITER

Diabetes, think of an ending. We open in three days.

ACTOR

Not me. I'm not opening in this turkey. I have a reputation as an actor, a following . . . My public expects to see me in a suitable vehicle.

WRITER

May I remind you, you're a starving, out-of-work actor

whom I've generously consented to let appear in my play in an effort to assist your comeback.

ACTOR

Starving, yes . . . Out of work, perhaps . . . Hoping for a comeback, maybe—but a drunkard?

WRITER

I never said you were a drunkard.

ACTOR

Yes, but I'm also a drunkard.

WRITER
(In a fit of sudden inspiration)
What if your character ripped a dagger from his robes and in a fit of frenzied frustration, tore away at his own eyes until he blinded himself?

ACTOR

Yeah, it's a great idea. Have you eaten anything today?

WRITER

What's wrong with it?

ACTOR

It's depressing. The audience will take one look at it and—

WRITER

I know—make that funny sound with their lips.

ACTOR

It's called hissing.

WRITER

Just once I want to win the competition! Once, before my life is over, I want my play to take first prize. And it's not the free case of ouzo I care about, it's the honor.

ACTOR
(Suddenly inspired)

What if the king suddenly changed his mind? There's a positive idea.

WRITER

He'd never do it.

ACTOR

(Selling him on it)

If the queen convinced him?

WRITER

She wouldn't. She's a bitch.

ACTOR

But if the Trojan Army surrendered—

WRITER

They'd fight to the death.

ACTOR

Not if Agamemnon reneged on his promise?

WRITER

It's not in his nature.

ACTOR

But I could suddenly take up arms and make a stand.

WRITER

It's against your character. You're a coward—an insignificant wretched slave with the intelligence of a worm. Why do you think I cast you?

ACTOR

I've just given you six possible endings!

WRITER

Each more clumsy than the last.

ACTOR

It's the play that's clumsy.

WRITER

Human beings don't behave that way. It's not in their nature.

ACTOR

What does their nature mean? We're stuck with a hopeless ending.

WRITER

As long as man is a rational animal, as a playwright, I cannot have a character do anything on stage he wouldn't do in real life.

ACTOR

May I remind you that we don't exist in real life.

WRITER

What do you mean?

ACTOR

You are aware that we're characters in a play right now in some Broadway theater? Don't get mad at me, I didn't write it.

WRITER

We're characters in a play and soon we're going to see my play . . . which is a play within a play. And they're watching us.

ACTOR

Yes. It's highly metaphysical, isn't it?

WRITER

Not only is it metaphysical, it's stupid!

ACTOR

Would you rather be one of them?

WRITER
(Looking at the audience)
Definitely not. Look at them.

ACTOR

Then let's get on with it!

WRITER
(Mutters)

They paid to get in.

ACTOR

Hepatitis, I'm talking to you!

WRITER

I know, the problem is the ending.

ACTOR

It's always the ending.

WRITER
(Suddenly to the audience)

Do you folks have any suggestions?

ACTOR

Stop talking to the audience! I'm sorry I mentioned them.

WRITER

It's bizarre, isn't it? We're two ancient Greeks in Athens
and we're about to see a play I wrote and you're acting in,
and they're from Queens or some terrible place like that
and they're watching us in someone else's play. What if
they're characters in another play? And someone's watching them? Or what if nothing exists and we're all in
somebody's dream? Or, what's worse, what if only that fat
guy in the third row exists?

ACTOR

That's my point. What if the universe is not rational and
people are not set things? Then we could change the ending
and it wouldn't have to conform to any fixed notions. You
follow me?

WRITER

Of course not. *(To the audience)* You follow him? He's an
actor. Eats at Sardi's.

ACTOR

Play characters would have no determined traits and could choose their own characters. I wouldn't have to be the slave just because you wrote it that way. I could choose to become a hero.

WRITER

Then there's no play.

ACTOR

No play? Good, I'll be at Sardi's.

WRITER

Diabetes, what you're suggesting is chaos!

ACTOR

Is freedom chaos?

WRITER

Is freedom chaos? Hmm . . . That's a toughie. *(To the audience)* Is freedom chaos? Did anybody out there major in philosophy?
(A GIRL from the audience answers)

GIRL

I did.

WRITER

Who's that?

GIRL

Actually I majored in gym, with a philosophy minor.

WRITER

Can you come up here?

ACTOR

What the hell are you doing?

GIRL

Does it matter if it was Brooklyn College?

WRITER

Brooklyn College? No, we'll take anything.
(She's made her way up)

ACTOR

I am really pissed off!

WRITER

What's eating you?

ACTOR

We're in the middle of a play. Who is she?

WRITER

In five minutes the Athenian Drama Festival begins, and I
have no ending for my play!

ACTOR

So?

WRITER

Serious philosophical questions have been raised. Do we
exist? Do they exist? *(Meaning the audience)* What is the true
nature of human character?

GIRL

Hi. I'm Doris Levine.

WRITER

I'm Hepatitis and this is Diabetes. We're ancient Greeks.

DORIS

I'm from Great Neck.

ACTOR

Get her off this stage!

WRITER
*(Really looking her up
and down, as she's lovely)*

She's very sexy.

ACTOR
What has that got to do with it?

DORIS
The basic philosophical question is: If a tree falls in the forest and no one is around to hear it—how do we know it makes a noise?
(Everyone looks around, puzzled over this)

ACTOR
Why do we care? We're on Forty-fifth Street.

WRITER
Will you go to bed with me?

ACTOR
Leave her alone!

DORIS
(To ACTOR)
Mind your own business.

WRITER
(Calling offstage)
Can we lower the curtain here? Just for five minutes
. . . *(To the audience)* Sit there. It'll be a quickie.

ACTOR
This is outrageous! It's absurd! *(To DORIS)* Do you have a friend?

DORIS
Sure. *(Calling to the audience)* Diane, you want to come up here . . . I got something going with a couple of Greeks. *(No response)* She's shy.

ACTOR
Well, we have a play to do. I'm going to report this to the author.

WRITER

I *am* the author!

ACTOR

I mean the original author.

WRITER

(Sotto voce to the ACTOR)

Diabetes, I think I can score with her.

ACTOR

What do you mean, score? You mean intercourse—with all these people watching?

WRITER

I'll lower the curtain. Some of them even do it. Not many, probably.

ACTOR

You idiot, you're fictional, she's Jewish—you know what the children will be like?

WRITER

Come on, maybe we can get her friend up here.

(The ACTOR goes to stage left to use the telephone)

Diane? This is a chance for a date with ————. *(Uses a real actor's name)* He's a big actor . . . lots of TV commercials . . .

ACTOR

(Into the phone)

Get me an outside line.

DORIS

I don't want to cause any trouble.

WRITER

It's no trouble. It's just that we've seemed to have lost touch with reality here.

DORIS

Who knows what reality really is?

WRITER

You're so right, Doris.

DORIS

(Philosophically)

So often people think they grasp reality when what they're really responding to is "fakeositude."

WRITER

I have an urge toward you that I'm sure is real.

DORIS

Is sex real?

WRITER

Even if it's not, it's still one of the best fake activities a person can do.

(He grabs her, she pulls back)

DORIS

Don't. Not here.

WRITER

Why not?

DORIS

I don't know. That's my line.

WRITER

Have you ever made it with a fictional character before?

DORIS

The closest I came was an Italian.

ACTOR

(He's on the phone. We hear the party on other end through a filter)

Hello?

PHONE
(Maid's voice)
Hello, Mr. Allen's residence.

ACTOR
Hello, may I speak to Mr. Allen?

MAID'S VOICE
Who's calling, please?

ACTOR
One of the characters in his play.

MAID
One second. Mr. Allen, there's a fictional character on the phone.

ACTOR
(To the others)
Now we'll see what happens with you lovebirds.

WOODY'S VOICE
Hello.

ACTOR
Mr. Allen?

WOODY
Yes?

ACTOR
This is Diabetes.

WOODY
Who?

ACTOR
Diabetes. I'm a character you created.

WOODY
Oh, yes . . . I remember, you're a badly drawn character . . . very one-dimensional.

ACTOR

Thanks.

WOODY

Hey—isn't the play on now?

ACTOR

That's what I'm calling about. We got a strange girl up on the stage and she won't get off and Hepatitis is suddenly hot for her.

WOODY

What does she look like?

ACTOR

She's pretty, but she doesn't belong.

WOODY

Blonde?

ACTOR

Brunette . . . long hair.

WOODY

Nice legs?

ACTOR

Yes.

WOODY

Good breasts?

ACTOR

Very nice.

WOODY

Keep her there, I'll be right over.

ACTOR

She's a philosophy student. But she's got no real answers . . . typical product of the Brooklyn College cafeteria.

WOODY

That's funny, I used that line in *Play It Again, Sam* to describe a girl.

ACTOR

I hope it got a better laugh there.

WOODY

Put her on.

ACTOR

On the phone?

WOODY

Sure.

ACTOR
(To DORIS)

It's for you.

DORIS
(Whispers)

I've seen him in the movies. Get rid of him.

ACTOR

He wrote the play.

DORIS

It's pretentious.

ACTOR
(Into the phone)

She won't speak to you. She says your play is pretentious.

WOODY

Oh, Jesus. Okay, call me back and let me know how the play ends.

ACTOR

Right.
(He hangs up, then does a double take, realizing what the author said)

DORIS

Can I have a part in your play?

ACTOR

I don't understand. Are you an actress or a girl playing an actress?

DORIS

I always wanted to be an actress. Mother hoped I'd become a nurse. Dad felt I should marry into society.

ACTOR

So what do you do for a living?

DORIS

I work for a company that makes deceptively shallow serving dishes for Chinese restaurants.
(A Greek enters from the wings)

TRICHINOSIS

Diabetes, Hepatitis. It's me, Trichinosis. *(Ad-lib greetings)* I have just come from a discussion with Socrates at the Acropolis and he proved that I didn't exist, so I'm upset. Still, word has it you need an ending for your play. I think I have just the thing.

WRITER

Really?

TRICHINOSIS

Who's she?

DORIS

Doris Levine.

TRICHINOSIS

Not from Great Neck?

DORIS

Yes.

TRICHINOSIS

You know the Rappaports?

DORIS

Myron Rappaport?

TRICHINOSIS
(Nodding)

We both worked for the Liberal party.

DORIS

What a coincidence.

TRICHINOSIS

You had an affair with Mayor Lindsay.

DORIS

I wanted to—he wouldn't.

WRITER

What's the ending?

TRICHINOSIS

You're much prettier than I imagined.

DORIS

Really?

TRICHINOSIS

I'd like to sleep with you right now.

DORIS

Tonight's my night. *(TRICHINOSIS takes her wrist passionately)* Please. I'm a virgin. Is that my line?
(The PROMPTER with book peeks out from the wings; is wearing a sweater)

PROMPTER

"Please. I'm a virgin." Yes.
(Exits)

WRITER

What's the goddamn ending?

TRICHINOSIS

Huh? Oh— *(Calls off)* Fellas!
(Some Greeks wheel out an elaborate machine)

WRITER

What the hell is that?

TRICHINOSIS

The ending for your play.

ACTOR

I don't understand.

TRICHINOSIS

This machine, which I've spent six months designing in my brother-in-law's shop, holds the answer.

WRITER

How?

TRICHINOSIS

In the final scene—when all looks black, and Diabetes the humble slave is in a position most hopeless—

ACTOR

Yes?

TRICHINOSIS

Zeus, Father of the Gods, descends dramatically from on high and brandishing his thunderbolts, brings salvation to a grateful but impotent group of mortals.

DORIS

Deus ex machina.

TRICHINOSIS

Hey—That's a great name for this thing!

DORIS

My father works for Westinghouse.

WRITER

I still don't get it.

TRICHINOSIS

Wait'll you see this thing in action. It flies Zeus in. I'm going to make a fortune with this invention. Sophocles put a deposit on one. Euripides wants two.

WRITER

But that changes the meaning of the play.

TRICHINOSIS

Don't speak till you see a demonstration. Bursitis, get into the flying harness.

BURSITIS

Me?

TRICHINOSIS

Do what I say. You won't believe this.

BURSITIS

I'm afraid of that thing.

TRICHINOSIS

He's kidding . . . Go ahead, you idiot, we're on the verge of a sale. He'll do it. Ha, ha . . .

BURSITIS

I don't like heights.

TRICHINOSIS

Get into it! Hurry up. Let's go! Get into your Zeus suit! A demonstration.
(Exiting as BURSITIS protests)

BURSITIS

I want to call my agent.

WRITER

But you're saying God comes in at the end and saves everything.

ACTOR

I love it! It gives the people their money's worth!

DORIS

He's right. It's like those Hollywood Bible movies.

WRITER
(Taking center stage a little too dramatically)
But if God saves everything, man is not responsible for his actions.

ACTOR

You wonder why you're not invited to more parties . . .

DORIS

But without God, the universe is meaningless. Life is meaningless. We're meaningless. *(Deadly pause)* I have a sudden and overpowering urge to get laid.

WRITER

Now I'm not in the mood.

DORIS

Really? Would anyone in the audience care to make it with me?

ACTOR

Stop that! *(To the audience)* She's not serious, folks.

WRITER

I'm depressed.

ACTOR

What's bothering you?

WRITER

I don't know if I believe in God.

DORIS
(To the audience)
I am serious.

ACTOR
If there's no God, who created the universe?

WRITER
I'm not sure yet.

ACTOR
Who do you mean, you're not sure yet!? When are you going to know?

DORIS
Anybody out there want to sleep with me?

MAN
(Rising in the audience)
I'll sleep with that girl if nobody else will.

DORIS
Will you, sir?

MAN
What's wrong with everybody? A beautiful girl like that? Aren't there any red-blooded men in the audience? You're all a bunch of New York left-wing Jewish intellectual commie pinkos—
(LORENZO MILLER comes out from wings. He is dressed in contemporary clothes)

LORENZO
Sit down, will you sit down?

MAN
Okay, okay.

WRITER
Who are you?

LORENZO

Lorenzo Miller. I created this audience. I'm a writer.

WRITER

What do you mean?

LORENZO

I wrote: a large group of people from Brooklyn, Queens, Manhattan, and Long Island come to the Golden Theater and watch a play. There they are.

DORIS
(Pointing to the audience)

You mean they're fictional too? *(LORENZO nods)* They're not free to do as they please?

LORENZO

They think they are, but they always do what's expected of them.

WOMAN
(Suddenly a WOMAN rises in audience, quite angrily)

I'm not fictional!

LORENZO

I'm sorry, madam, but you are.

WOMAN

But I have a son at the Harvard Business School.

LORENZO

I created your son; he's fictional. Not only is he fictional, he's homosexual.

MAN

I'll show you how fictional I am. I'm leaving this theater and getting my money back. This is a stupid play. In fact, it's no play. I go to the theater, I want to see something with a story—with a beginning, middle, and end—instead of this bullshit. Good night.
(Exits up the aisle in a huff)

LORENZO
(To the audience)
Isn't he a great character. I wrote him very angry. Later he feels guilty and commits suicide. *(Sound: gunshot)* Later!

MAN
(Reenters with a smoking pistol)
I'm sorry, did I do it too soon?

LORENZO
Get out of here!

MAN
I'll be at Sardi's.
(Exits)

LORENZO
(In the audience, dealing with various people of the actual audience)
What's your name, sir? Uh-huh. *(Ad-lib section, depending on what audience says)* Where are you from? Isn't he cute? Great character. Must remind them to dress him differently. Later this woman leaves her husband for this guy. Hard to believe, I know. Oh—look at this guy. Later he rapes that lady.

WRITER
It's terrible being fictional. We're all so limited.

LORENZO
Only by the limits of the playwright. Unfortunately you happen to have been written by Woody Allen. Think if you were written by Shakespeare.

WRITER
I don't accept it. I'm a free man and I don't need God flying in to save my play. I'm a good writer.

DORIS
You want to win the Athenian Drama Festival, don't you?

WRITER

(Suddenly dramatic)

Yes. I want to be immortal. I don't want to just die and be forgotten. I want my works to live on long after my physical body has passed away. I want future generations to know I existed! Please don't let me be a meaningless dot, drifting through eternity. I thank you, ladies and gentlemen. I would like to accept this Tony Award and thank David Merrick . . .

DORIS

I don't care what anybody says, I'm real.

LORENZO

Not really.

DORIS

I think, therefore I am. Or better yet, I *feel*—I have an orgasm.

LORENZO

You do?

DORIS

All the time.

LORENZO

Really?

DORIS

Very frequently.

LORENZO

Yes?

DORIS

Most of the time I do, yes.

LORENZO

Yes?

DORIS

At least half the time.

LORENZO

No.

DORIS

I do! With certain men . . .

LORENZO

Hard to believe.

DORIS

Not necessarily through intercourse. Usually it's oral—

LORENZO

Uh-huh.

DORIS

Of course I fake it too. I don't want to insult anybody.

LORENZO

Have you ever had an orgasm?

DORIS

Not really. No.

LORENZO

Because none of us are real.

WRITER

But if we're not real, we can't die.

LORENZO

No. Not unless the playwright decides to kill us.

WRITER

Why would he do something like that?
(*From the wings, BLANCHE DuBOIS enters*)

BLANCHE

Because, sugar, it satisfies something called their—aesthetic
sensibility.

WRITER
(All turn to look at her)

Who are you?

DORIS

BLANCHE

Blanche. Blanche DuBois. It means "white woods." Don't get up, please—I was just passing through.

DORIS

What are you doing here?

BLANCHE

Seeking refuge. Yes—in this old theater . . . I couldn't help overhearing your conversation. Could I get a coke with a little bourbon in it?

ACTOR
(Appears. We didn't realize he'd slipped away)

Is a Seven-Up okay?

WRITER

Where the hell were you?

ACTOR

I went to the bathroom.

WRITER

In the middle of the play?

ACTOR

What play? *(To BLANCHE)* Will you explain to him we're all limited.

BLANCHE

I'm afraid it's all too true. Too true and too ghastly. That's why I ran out of my play. Escaped. Oh, not that Mr. Tennessee Williams is not a very great writer, but honey— he dropped me in the center of a nightmare. The last thing I remember, I was being taken out by two strangers, one who held a strait jacket. Once outside the Kowalski

residence, I broke free and ran. I've got to get into another
play, a play where God exists . . . somewhere where I can
rest at last. That's why you must put me in your play and
allow Zeus, young and handsome Zeus to triumph with his
thunderbolt.

WRITER

You went to the bathroom?

TRICHINOSIS
(Enters)

Ready for the demonstration.

BLANCHE

A demonstration. How wonderful.

TRICHINOSIS
(Calling offstage)

Ready out there? Okay. It's the end of the play. Everything
looks hopeless for the slave. All other means desert him. He
prays. Go ahead.

ACTOR

Oh, Zeus. Great god. We are confused and helpless mortals.
Please be merciful and change our lives. *(Nothing happens)*
Er . . . great Zeus . . .

TRICHINOSIS

Let's go, fellas! For Christ's sake.

ACTOR

Oh, great God.
*(Suddenly there is thunder and fabulous lightning. The effect is
wonderful: ZEUS descends, hurling thunderbolts majestically)*

BURSITIS
(As ZEUS)

I am Zeus, God of Gods! Worker of miracles! Creator of the
universe! I bring salvation to all!

DORIS

Wait'll Westinghouse sees this!

TRICHINOSIS

Well, Hepatitis, what do you think?

WRITER

I love it! It's better than I expected. It's dramatic, it's flamboyant. I'm going to win the festival! I'm a winner. It's so religious. Look, I got chills! Doris!

(He grabs her)

DORIS

Not now.

(There is a general exit, a light change . . .)

WRITER

I must do some immediate rewrites.

TRICHINOSIS

I'll rent you my God machine for twenty-six fifty an hour.

WRITER

(To LORENZO)

Can you introduce my play?

LORENZO

Sure, go ahead. *(THEY all exit. LORENZO stays behind and faces audience. As he speaks, a Greek CHORUS enters and sits in the background of the amphitheater. White-robed, naturally)* Good evening and welcome to the Athenian Drama Festival. *(Sound: cheering)* We got a great show for you tonight. A new play by Hepatitis of Rhodes, entitled, "The Slave." *(Sound: cheers)* Starring Diabetes as the slave, with Bursitis as Zeus, Blanche DuBois, and Doris Levine from Great Neck. *(Cheers)* The show is brought to you by Gregory Londos' Lamb Restaurant, just opposite the Parthenon. Don't be a Medusa with snakes in *your* hair when you're looking for a place to dine out. Try Gregory Londos' Lamb Restaurant. Remember, Homer liked it—and he was blind.

(He exits. DIABETES plays the slave named PHIDIPIDES and right now, he drifts on with another GREEK SLAVE as the CHORUS takes over)

CHORUS

Gather round, ye Greeks, and heed the story of Phidipides —one so wise, so passionate, so steeped in the glories of Greece.

DIABETES

My point is, what are we going to do with such a big horse?

FRIEND

But they want to give it to us for nothing.

DIABETES

So what? Who needs it? It's a big wooden horse . . . What the hell are we going to do with it? It's not even a pretty horse. Mark my words, Cratinus—as a Greek statesman, I would never trust the Trojans. You notice they never take a day off?

FRIEND

Did you hear about Cyclops? He got a middle eye infection.

VOICE OFF

Phidipides! Where is that slave?

DIABETES

Coming, Master!

MASTER
(Enters)

Phidipides—there you are. There's work to be done. The grapes need picking, my chariot must be repaired, we need water from the well—and you're out shmoozing.

DIABETES

I wasn't shmoozing, Master, I was discussing politics.

MASTER

A slave discussing politics! Ha, ha!

CHORUS

Ha, ha . . . That's rich.

DIABETES

I'm sorry, Master.

MASTER

You and the new Hebrew slave clean the house. I'm expecting guests. Then get on with all the other tasks.

DIABETES

The new Hebrew?

MASTER

Doris Levine.

DORIS

You called?

MASTER

Clean up. Let's go. Hurry on.

CHORUS

Poor Phidipides. A slave. And like all slaves, he longed for one thing.

DIABETES

To be taller.

CHORUS

To be free.

DIABETES

I don't want to be free.

CHORUS

No?

DIABETES

I like it this way. I know what's expected of me. I'm taken

care of. I don't have to make any choices. I was born a slave and I'll die a slave. I have no anxiety.

CHORUS

Boo . . . boo . . .

DIABETES

Ah, what do you know, chorus boys.
(He kisses DORIS, she pulls away)

DORIS

Don't.

DIABETES

Why not? Doris, you know my heart is heavy with love—or as you Hebrews are fond of saying, I have a thing for you.

DORIS

It can't work.

DIABETES

Why not?

DORIS

Because you like being a slave and I hate it. I want my freedom. I want to travel and write books, live in Paris, maybe start a woman's magazine.

DIABETES

What's the big deal about freedom? It's dangerous. To know one's place is safe. Don't you see, Doris, governments change hands every week, political leaders murder one another, cities are sacked, people are tortured. If there's a war, who do you think gets killed? The free people. But we're safe because no matter who's in power, they all need someone to do the heavy cleaning.
(He grabs her)

DORIS

Don't. While I am still a slave I can never enjoy sex.

DIABETES

Would you be willing to fake it?

DORIS

Forget it.

CHORUS

And then one day the fates lent a hand.
(The FATES enter, a couple dressed like American tourists, wearing jazzy Hawaiian shirts; BOB has a camera around his neck)

BOB

Hi, we're the Fates, Bob and Wendy Fate. We need someone to take an urgent message to the king.

DIABETES

The king?

BOB

You would be doing mankind a great service.

DIABETES

I would?

WENDY

Yes, but it's a dangerous mission, and even though you are a slave, you may say no.

DIABETES

No.

BOB

But it will give you a chance to see the palace in all its glory.

WENDY

And the reward is your freedom.

DIABETES

My freedom? Yes, well, I'd love to help you, but I have a roast in the stove.

DORIS

Let me do it.

BOB

It's too dangerous for a woman.

DIABETES

She's a very fast runner.

DORIS

Phidipides, how can you refuse?

DIABETES

When you're a coward, certain things come easy.

WENDY

We beg of you—please—

BOB

The fate of mankind hangs in the balance.

WENDY

We'll raise the reward. Freedom for you and any person of
your choice.

BOB

Plus a sixteen-piece starter set of silverware.

DORIS

Phidipides, here's our chance.

CHORUS

Go ahead, you jerk.

DIABETES

A dangerous mission followed by personal freedom? I'm
getting nauseous.

WENDY
(Hands him an envelope)
Take this message to the king.

DIABETES

Why can't you take it?

BOB

We're leaving for New York in a few hours.

DORIS

Phidipides, you say you love me—

DIABETES

I do.

CHORUS

Let's go, Phidipides, the play is bogging down.

DIABETES

Decisions, decisions . . . *(The phone rings, and he answers it)*
Hello?

WOODY'S VOICE

Will you take the goddamn message to the king. We'd all
like to get the hell out of here.

DIABETES
(Hangs up)
I'll do it. But only because Woody asked me to.

CHORUS
(Sings)
Poor Professor Higgins—

DIABETES

That's the wrong show, you idiots!

DORIS

Good luck, Phidipides.

WENDY

You're really going to need it.

DIABETES

What do you mean?

WENDY

Bob here is really a practical joker.

DORIS

After we're free we can go to bed, and maybe for once I'll enjoy it.

HEPATITIS

(Pops on stage)

Sometimes a little grass before you make it—

ACTOR

You're the writer!

HEPATITIS

I couldn't resist!

(Exit)

DORIS

Go!

DIABETES

I'm going!

CHORUS

And so Phidipides set out on his journey, bearing an important message for King Oedipus.

DIABETES

King Oedipus?

CHORUS

Yes.

DIABETES

I hear he lives with his mother.

(Effects: Wind and lightning as SLAVE trudges on)

CHORUS

Over deep mountains, through high valleys.

DIABETES

High mountains and deep valleys. Where did we get this chorus?

CHORUS

At all times at the mercy of the Furies.

DIABETES

The Furies are having dinner with the Fates. They went to Chinatown. The Hong Fat Noodle Company.

HEPATITIS
(Enters)

Sam Wo's is better.

DIABETES

There's always a line at Sam Wo's.

CHORUS

Not if you ask for Lee. He'll seat you, but you have to tip him.

(HEPATITIS exits)

DIABETES
(Proudly)

Yesterday I was a lousy slave, never having ventured beyond my master's property. Today I carry a message to the king, the king himself. I see the world. Soon I'll be a free man. Suddenly human possibilities are opening up to me. And because of it—I have an uncontrollable urge to throw up. Oh, well . . .

(Wind)

CHORUS

Days turn into weeks, weeks into months. Still Phidipides struggles on.

DIABETES

Can you turn off the goddamn wind machine?

CHORUS

Poor Phidipides, mortal man.

DIABETES

I'm tired, I'm weary, I'm sick. I can't go on. My hand is shaking . . . *(The CHORUS begins humming a slow version of "Dixie")* All around me men dying, war and misery, brother against brother; the South, rich in tradition; the North, mostly industrial. President Lincoln, sending the Union Army to destroy the plantation. The Old Homestead. Cotton—comin' down the river . . . *(HEPATITIS enters and stares at him)* Lawsy, lawsy, Miss Eva—Ah can't cross the ice. It's General Beauregard and Robert E. Lee . . . Ah— *(Notices HEPATITIS staring at him)* I—I . . . I got carried away.
(HEPATITIS grabs him around the neck and pulls him to the side)

HEPATITIS

C'mere! What the hell are you doing!?

DIABETES

Where's the palace? I'm walking around for days! What kind of play is this!? Where the hell is the goddamn palace? In Bensonhurst?

HEPATITIS

You're at the palace if you'd stop ruining my play! Guard! Come on now, shape up.
(A powerful GUARD enters)

GUARD

Who are you?

DIABETES

Phidipides.

GUARD

What brings you to the palace?

DIABETES

The palace? I'm here?

GUARD

Yes. This is the royal palace. The most beautiful structure in all of Greece, marble, majestic, and completely rent-controlled.

DIABETES

I bear a message for the king.

GUARD

Oh, yes. He is expecting you.

DIABETES

My throat is parched and I have not eaten in days.

GUARD

I will summon the king.

DIABETES

What about a roast-beef sandwich?

GUARD

I will get the king and a roast-beef sandwich. How do you want that?

DIABETES

Medium.

GUARD
(Takes out a pad and writes)
One medium. You get a vegetable with that.

DIABETES

What do you have?

GUARD

Let's see, today . . . carrots or baked potato.

DIABETES

I'll have the baked potato.

GUARD

Coffee?

DIABETES

Please. And a toasted bow tie—if you have one—and the king.

GUARD

Right. *(As he exits)* Let me have an RB to go with a regular coffee.

(The FATES cross, taking pictures)

BOB

How do you like the palace?

DIABETES

I love it.

BOB

(Handing his wife the camera)
Take one of us together.

(As she does)

DIABETES

I thought you two were going back to New York.

WENDY

You know how fate is.

BOB

Unreliable. Take it easy.

DIABETES

(Leans in to smell the flower in BOB's lapel)
That's a pretty flower.
(Gets an eyeful of water as FATES laugh)

BOB

I'm sorry, I couldn't resist.
(Offers his hand. DIABETES shakes it. Gets a shock from a joy buzzer)

DIABETES

Ahhhh!

(FATES exit laughing)

WENDY

He loves to play tricks on people.

DIABETES

(To CHORUS)

You knew he was out to get me.

CHORUS

He's a scream.

DIABETES

Why didn't you warn me?

CHORUS

We don't like to get involved.

DIABETES

You don't like to get involved? You know, a woman was stabbed to death on the BMT while sixteen people looked on and didn't help.

CHORUS

We read it in the *Daily News*, and it was the IRT.

DIABETES

If one person had the guts to help her, maybe she'd be here today.

WOMAN

(Enters with knife in her chest)

I am here.

DIABETES

I had to open my mouth.

WOMAN

A woman works her whole life on DeKalb Ave. I'm reading the *Post*, six hooligans—dope addicts—grab me and throw me down.

CHORUS

There weren't six, there were three.

WOMAN

Three, six—they had a knife, they wanted my money.

DIABETES

You should have given it to them.

WOMAN

I did. They still stabbed me.

CHORUS

That's New York. You give 'em the money and they still stab you.

DIABETES

New York? It's everywhere. I was walking with Socrates in downtown Athens, and two youths from Sparta jump out from behind the Acropolis and want all our money.

WOMAN

What happened?

DIABETES

Socrates proved to them using simple logic that evil was merely ignorance of the truth.

WOMAN

And?

DIABETES

And they broke his nose.

WOMAN

I just hope your message for the king is good news.

DIABETES

I hope so, for his sake.

WOMAN

For your sake.

DIABETES

Right and—what do you mean, for my sake?

CHORUS
(Derisively)

Ha, ha, ha!
(The light becomes more ominous)

DIABETES

The light is changing . . . What is that? What happens if
it's bad news?

WOMAN

In ancient times, when a messenger brought a message to
the king, if the news was good, the messenger received a
reward.

CHORUS

Free passes to the Loew's Eighty-sixth Street.

WOMAN

But if the news was bad . . .

DIABETES

Don't tell me.

WOMAN

The king would have the messenger put to death.

DIABETES

Are we in ancient times?

WOMAN

Can't you tell by what you're wearing?

DIABETES

I see what you mean. Hepatitis!

WOMAN

Sometimes the messenger would have his head cut off . . . if
the king was in a forgiving mood.

DIABETES

A forgiving mood, he cuts your head off?

CHORUS

But if the news is really bad—

WOMAN

Then the messenger is roasted to death—

CHORUS

Over a slow fire.

DIABETES

It's been so long since I've been roasted over a slow fire, I can't remember if I like it or not.

CHORUS

Take our word for it—you won't like it.

DIABETES

Where's Doris Levine? If I get my hands on that Hebrew slave from Great Neck . . .

WOMAN

She can't help you, she's miles away.

DIABETES

Doris! Where the hell are you?

DORIS
(In the audience)

What do you want?

DIABETES

What are you doing there?

DORIS

I got bored with the play.

DIABETES

What do you mean, you got bored? Get up here! I'm up to my ass in trouble because of you!

DORIS
(Coming up)

I'm sorry, Phidipides, how did I know what happened in ancient history? I studied philosophy.

DIABETES

If the news is bad, I die.

DORIS

I heard her.

DIABETES

Is this your idea of freedom?

DORIS

Win a couple, lose a couple.

DIABETES

Win a couple, lose a couple? That's what they teach you at Brooklyn College?

DORIS

Hey, man, get off my back.

DIABETES

If the news is bad I'm finished. Wait a minute! The news! The message. I got it right here! *(Fumbles, takes a message from an envelope. Reads)* For Best Supporting Actor, the winner is ———. *(Use the name of the actor playing HEPATITIS)*

HEPATITIS
(Pops on)

I want to accept this Tony Award and thank David Merrick—

ACTOR

Get off, I read the wrong message!
(Pulls out the real one)

WOMAN

Hurry, the king's coming.

DIABETES

See if he has my sandwich.

DORIS

Hurry, Phidipides!

DIABETES
(Reads)

The message is one word.

DORIS

Yes?

DIABETES

How'd you know?

DORIS

Know what?

DIABETES

What the message is, it's "yes."

CHORUS

Is that good or bad?

DIABETES

Yes? Yes is affirmative? No? Isn't it? *(Testing it)* *Yes!*

DORIS

What if the question is, Does the queen have the clap?

DIABETES

I see your point.

CHORUS

His majesty, the king!
(Fanfare, big entrance of KING)

DIABETES

Sire, does the queen have the clap?

KING

Who ordered this roast beef?

DIABETES

I did, sire. Is that carrots? Because I asked for a baked potato.

KING

We're out of baked potatoes.

DIABETES

Then take it back. I'll go across the street.

CHORUS

The message. *(DIABETES keeps shhing them)* The message, he has the message.

KING

Humble slave, do you have a message for me?

DIABETES

Humble king, er , . . yes, as a matter of fact . . .

KING

Good.

DIABETES

Can you tell me the question?

KING

First the message.

DIABETES

No, you first.

KING

No, you.

DIABETES

No, you.

KING

No, you.

CHORUS

Make Phidipides go first.

KING

Him?

CHORUS

Yes.

KING

How can I?

CHORUS

Shmuck, you're the king.

KING

Of course, I'm the king. What is the message?
(The GUARD draws a sword)

DIABETES

The message is . . . ye-no—*(Trying to get an idea before spilling it)* no-yeah—maybe—maybe—

CHORUS

He's lying.

KING

The message, slave.
(The GUARD puts a sword to DIABETES' throat)

DIABETES

It is one word, sire.

KING

One word?

DIABETES

Amazing, isn't it, because for the same money he's allowed fourteen words.

KING

A one-word answer to my question of questions. Is there a god?

DIABETES

That's the question?

KING

That—is the only question.

DIABETES
(Looks at DORIS, relieved)
Then I'm proud to give you the message. The word is yes.

KING

Yes?

DIABETES

Yes.

CHORUS

Yes.

DORIS

Yes.

DIABETES

Your turn.

WOMAN
(Lisp)

Yeth.
(DIABETES gives her an annoyed look)

DORIS

Isn't that fabulous!

DIABETES

I know what you're thinking, a little reward for your faithful messenger—but our freedom is more than enough—on the other hand, if you insist on showing your appreciation, I think diamonds are always in good taste.

KING
(Gravely)

If there is a god, then man is not responsible and I will surely be judged for my sins.

DIABETES
Pardon me?

KING
Judged for my sins, my crimes. Very horrible crimes, I am doomed. This message you bring me dooms me for eternity.

DIABETES
Did I say yes? I meant no.

GUARD
(Seizes the envelope and reads the message)
The message is yes, sire.

KING
This is the worst possible news.

DIABETES
(Dropping to his knees)
Sire, it's not my fault. I'm a lowly messenger, I don't create the message. I merely transmit it. It's like her majesty's clap.

KING
You will be torn apart by wild horses.

DIABETES
I knew you'd understand.

DORIS
But he's only the messenger. You can't have him torn apart by wild horses. You usually roast them over a slow fire.

KING
Too good for this scum!

DIABETES
When the weatherman predicts rain, do you kill the weatherman?

KING

Yes.

DIABETES

I see. Well. I'm dealing with a schizophrenic.

KING

Seize him.
(The GUARD does)

DIABETES

Wait, sire. A word in my defense.

KING

Yes?

DIABETES

This is only a play.

KING

That's what they all say. Give me your sword. I want the pleasure of this kill myself.

DORIS

No, no—oh, why did I get us into this?

CHORUS

Don't worry, you're young, you'll find somebody else.

DORIS

That's true.

KING
(Raises the sword)

Die!

DIABETES

Oh, Zeus—God of Gods, come forward with your thunder-bolt and save me— *(All look up; nothing happens, awkward moment)* Oh, Zeus . . . Oh, Zeus!!!

KING

And now—die!

DIABETES

Oh, Zeus—where the hell is Zeus!

HEPATITIS
(He enters and looks up)
For Christ's sake, let's go with the machine! Lower him!

TRICHINOSIS
(Enters from the other side)
It's stuck!

DIABETES
(Giving the cue again)
Oh, great Zeus!

CHORUS
All men come to the same end.

WOMAN
I'm not gonna stand here and let him get stabbed like I was on the BMT!

KING
Grab her.
(The GUARD grabs her and stabs her)

WOMAN
That's twice this week! Son of a bitch.

DIABETES
Oh, great Zeus! God, help me!
(Effect. Lightning—ZEUS is lowered very clumsily and he jerks around until we see the lowering wire has strangled him. Everyone looks on, stunned)

TRICHINOSIS
Something's wrong with the machine! It's out of joint.

CHORUS

At last, the entrance of God!
(But he's definitely dead)

DIABETES

God . . . God? God? God, are you okay? Is there a doctor
in the house?

DOCTOR
(In the audience)

I'm a doctor.

TRICHINOSIS

The machine got screwed up.

HEPATITIS

Psst. Get off. You're ruining the play.

DIABETES

God is dead.

DOCTOR

Is he covered by anything?

HEPATITIS

Ad-lib.

DIABETES

What?

HEPATITIS

Ad-lib the ending.

TRICHINOSIS

Somebody pulled the wrong lever.

DORIS

His neck is broken.

KING
(Trying to continue the play)

Er . . . well, messenger . . . see what you've done.
(Brandishes the sword. DIABETES grabs it)

DIABETES
(Grabbing sword)
I'll take that.

KING
What the hell are you doing?

DIABETES
Kill me, eh? Doris, get over here.

KING
Phidipides, what are you doing?

GUARD
Hepatitis, he's ruining the end.

CHORUS
What're you doing, Phidipides? The king should kill *you*.

DIABETES
Says who? Where is it written? No—I choose to kill the king.
(Stabs the KING, but the sword is fake)

KING
Leave me alone . . . He's crazy . . . Stop! . . . That tickles.

DOCTOR
(Taking the pulse of the body of GOD)
He's definitely dead. We better move him.

CHORUS
We don't want to get involved.
(THEY start exiting, carrying GOD off)

DIABETES
The slave decides to be a hero!
(Stabs the GUARD; the sword is still a fake)

GUARD
What the hell are you doing?

DORIS

I love you, Phidipides. *(He kisses her.)* Please, I'm not in the mood.

HEPATITIS

My play . . . my play! *(To CHORUS)* Where are you going?

KING

I'm going to call my agent at the William Morris Agency. Sol Mishkin. He'll know what to do.

HEPATITIS

This is a very serious play with a message! If it falls apart, they'll never get the message.

WOMAN

The theater is for entertainment. There's an old saying, if you want to send a message, call Western Union.

WESTERN UNION DELIVERY BOY
(Enters on a bicycle)

I have a telegram for the audience. It's the author's message.

DIABETES

Who's he?

DELIVERY BOY
(Dismounts, sings)

Happy birthday to you, happy birthday to you—

HEPATITIS

It's the wrong message!

DELIVERY BOY
(Reads the wire)

I'm sorry, here it is. God is dead. Stop. You're on your own. And it's signed—The Moscowitz Billiard Ball Company?

DIABETES

Of course anything is possible. I'm the hero now.

DORIS

And I just know I'm going to have an orgasm. I know it.

DELIVERY BOY
(Still reads)

Doris Levine can definitely have an orgasm. Stop. If she wants to. Stop.

(He grabs her)

DORIS

Stop.
(In the background a brutish man enters)

STANLEY

Stella! Stella!

HEPATITIS

There is no more reality! Absolutely none.
(GROUCHO MARX runs across stage chasing BLANCHE. A MAN in audience rises)

MAN

If anything's possible, I'm not going home to Forest Hills! I'm tired of working on Wall Street. I'm sick of the Long Island Expressway!
(Grabs a WOMAN in the audience. Rips her blouse off, chases her up the aisle. This could also be an usherette)

HEPATITIS

My play . . . *(The characters have left the stage, leaving the two original characters, the author and actor, HEPATITIS and DIABE-TES)* My play . . .

DIABETES

It was a good play. All it needed was an ending.

HEPATITIS

But what did it mean?

DIABETES

Nothing . . . just nothing . . .

HEPATITIS

What?

DIABETES

Meaningless. It's empty.

HEPATITIS

The ending.

DIABETES

Of course. What are we discussing? We're discussing the ending.

HEPATITIS

We're always discussing the ending.

DIABETES

Because it's hopeless.

HEPATITIS

I admit it's unsatisfying.

DIABETES

Unsatisfying!? It's not even believable. *(The lights start dimming)* The trick is to start at the ending when you write a play. Get a good, strong ending, and then write backwards.

HEPATITIS

I've tried that. I got a play with no beginning.

DIABETES

That's absurd.

HEPATITIS

Absurd? What's absurd?
(BLACKOUT)

Fabulous Tales and Mythical Beasts

(The following is a sample of some of world literature's more imaginative creations that I am anthologizing in a four-volume set that Remainder and Sons plans to publish pending the outcome of the Norwegian shepherds' strike.)

THE NURK

The nurk is a bird two inches long that has the power of speech but keeps referring to itself in the third person, such as, "He's a great little bird, isn't he?"

Persian mythology holds that if a nurk appears on the window sill in the morning a relative will either come into money or break both legs at a raffle.

Zoroaster was said to have received a nurk as a gift on his birthday, although what he really needed was some gray slacks. The nurk also appears in Babylonian mythology, but here he is much more sarcastic and is always saying, "Ah, come off it."

Some readers may be acquainted with a lesser-known opera by Holstein called *Taffelspitz*, in which a mute girl falls in love with a nurk, kisses it, and they both fly around the room till the curtain falls.

THE FLYING SNOLL
· · · · · · · · · · ·

A lizard with four hundred eyes, two hundred for distance
and two hundred for reading. According to legend, if a man
gazes directly into the face of the snoll he immediately loses
his right to drive in New Jersey.

Also legendary is the snoll's graveyard, the location of
which is unknown even to snolls, and should a snoll drop
dead he must remain where he is until picked up.

In Norse mythology, Loki attempts to find the snoll's
graveyard but chances upon some Rhine maidens bathing
instead and somehow winds up with trichinosis.

· · ·

The Emperor Ho Sin had a dream in which he beheld a
palace greater than his for half the rent. Stepping through
the portals of the edifice, Ho Sin suddenly found that his
body became young again, although his head remained
somewhere between sixty-five and seventy. Opening a door,
he found another door, which led to another; soon he
realized he had entered a hundred doors and was now out
in the backyard.

Just when Ho Sin was on the verge of despair, a
nightingale perched on his shoulder and sang the most
beautiful song he'd ever heard and then bit him on the nose.

Chastened, Ho Sin looked into a mirror and instead of
seeing his own reflection, he saw a man named Mendel
Goldblatt who worked for the Wasserman Plumbing Company and who accused him of taking his overcoat.

From this Ho Sin learned the secret of life, and it was
"Never to yodel."

When the emperor awoke he was in a cold sweat and
couldn't recall if he dreamed the dream or was now in a
dream being dreamt by his bail bondsman.

THE FREAN
. . . .

The frean is a sea monster with the body of a crab and the head of a certified public accountant.

Freans are said to possess fine singing voices which drive sailors mad when they hear them, particularly on Cole Porter tunes.

Killing a frean is bad luck: in a poem by Sir Herbert Figg, a sailor shoots one and his boat suddenly founders in a storm, causing the crew to seize the captain and jettison his false teeth in hopes of staying afloat.

THE GREAT ROE
. . . .

The great roe is a mythological beast with the head of a lion and the body of a lion, though not the same lion. The roe is reputed to sleep for a thousand years and then suddenly rise in flames, particularly if it was smoking when it dozed off.

Odysseus was said to have awakened a roe after six hundred years but found it listless and grouchy, and it begged to remain in bed just two hundred more years.

The appearance of a Roe is generally considered unlucky and usually precedes a famine or news of a cocktail party.

. . .

A wise man in India bet a magician that he could not fool him, whereupon the magician tapped the wise man on the head and changed him into a dove. The dove then flew out the window to Madagascar and had his luggage forwarded.

The wise man's wife, who had witnessed this, asked the magician if he could also change things to gold, and if so, could he change her brother to three dollars in cash so the whole day shouldn't be a total loss.

The magician said that in order to learn that trick one must journey to the four corners of the earth, but that one should go in the off-season, as three of the corners are usually booked.

The woman thought a moment and then set out on a pilgrimage to Mecca, forgetting to turn off her stove. Seventeen years later she returned, having spoken with the High Lama, and immediately went on welfare.

(The above is one of a series of Hindu myths that explain why we have wheat. Author.)

THE WEAL
. . . .

A large white mouse with the lyrics to "Am I Blue?" printed on its stomach.

The weal is unique amongst rodents in that it can be picked up and played like an accordion. Similar to the weal is the lunette, a small squirrel that can whistle and knows the mayor of Detroit personally.

. . .

Astronomers talk of an inhabited planet named Quelm, so distant from earth that a man traveling at the speed of light would take six million years to get there, although they are planning a new express route that will cut two hours off the trip.

Since the temperature on Quelm is thirteen hundred below, bathing is not permitted and the resorts have either closed down or now feature live entertainment.

Because of its remoteness from the center of the solar system, gravity is nonexistent on Quelm and having a large sit-down dinner takes a great deal of planning.

In addition to all these obstacles on Quelm, there is no oxygen to support life as we know it, and what creatures do exist find it hard to earn a living without holding down two jobs.

Legend has it, however, that many billions of years ago the environment was not quite so horrible—or at least no worse than Pittsburgh—and that human life existed. These humans—resembling men in every way except perhaps for a large head of lettuce where the nose normally is—were to a man philosophers. As philosophers they relied heavily on logic and felt that if life existed, somebody must have caused it, and they went looking for a dark-haired man with a tattoo who was wearing a Navy pea jacket.

When nothing materialized, they abandoned philosophy and went into the mail-order business, but postal rates went up and they perished.

But Soft...
Real Soft

Ask the average man who wrote the plays entitled *Hamlet*, *Romeo and Juliet*, *King Lear*, and *Othello*, and in most cases he'll snap confidently back with, "The Immortal Bard of Stratford on Avon." Ask him about the authorship of the Shakespearean sonnets and see if you don't get the same illogical reply. Now put these questions to certain literary detectives who seem to crop up every now and again over the years, and don't be surprised if you get answers like Sir Francis Bacon, Ben Jonson, Queen Elizabeth and possibly even the Homestead Act.

The most recent of these theories is to be found in a book I have just read that attempts to prove conclusively that the real author of Shakespeare's works was Christopher Marlowe. The book makes a very convincing case, and when I got through reading it I was not sure if Shakespeare was Marlowe or Marlowe was Shakespeare or what. I know this, I would not have cashed checks for either one of them—and I like their work.

Now, in trying to keep the above mentioned theory in perspective, my first question is: if Marlowe wrote Shakespeare's works, who wrote Marlowe's? The answer to this lies in the fact that Shakespeare was married to a woman named Anne Hathaway. This we know to be factual. However, under the new theory, it is actually Marlowe who was married to Anne Hathaway, a match which caused Shakespeare no end of grief, as they would not let him in the house.

One fateful day, in a jealous rage over who held the lower number in a bakery, Marlowe was slain—slain or whisked away in disguise to avoid charges of heresy, a most serious crime punishable by slaying or whisking away or both.

It was at this point that Marlowe's young wife took up the pen and continued to write the plays and sonnets we all know and avoid today. But allow me to clarify.

We all realize Shakespeare (Marlowe) borrowed his plots from the ancients (moderns); however, when the time came to return the plots to the ancients he had used them up and was forced to flee the country under the assumed name of William Bard (hence the term "immortal bard") in an effort to avoid debtor's prison (hence the term "debtor's prison"). Here Sir Francis Bacon enters into the picture. Bacon was an innovator of the times who was working on advanced concepts of refrigeration. Legend has it he died attempting to refrigerate a chicken. Apparently the chicken pushed first. In an effort to conceal Marlowe from Shakespeare, should they prove to be the same person, Bacon had adopted the fictitious name Alexander Pope, who in reality was Pope Alexander, head of the Roman Catholic Church and currently in exile owing to the invasion of Italy by the Bards, last of the nomadic hordes (the Bards give us the term "immortal bard"), and years before had galloped off to London, where Raleigh awaited death in the tower.

The mystery deepens for, as this goes on, Ben Jonson stages a mock funeral for Marlowe, convincing a minor poet to take his place for the burial. Ben Jonson is not to be confused with Samuel Johnson. He was Samuel Johnson. Samuel Johnson was not. Samuel Johnson was Samuel

Pepys. Pepys was actually Raleigh, who had escaped from the tower to write *Paradise Lost* under the name of John Milton, a poet who because of blindness accidentally escaped to the tower and was hanged under the name of Jonathan Swift. This all becomes clearer when we realize that George Eliot was a woman.

Proceeding from this then, King Lear is not a play by Shakespeare but a satirical revue by Chaucer, originally titled "Nobody's Parfit," which contains in it a clue to the man who killed Marlowe, a man known around Elizabethan times (Elizabeth Barret Browning) as Old Vic. Old Vic became more familiar to us later as Victor Hugo, who wrote *The Hunchback of Notre Dame*, which most students of literature feel is merely *Coriolanus* with a few obvious changes. (Say them both fast.)

We wonder then, was not Lewis Carroll caricaturing the whole situation when he wrote *Alice in Wonderland?* The March Hare was Shakespeare, the Mad Hatter, Marlowe, and the Dormouse, Bacon—or the Mad Hatter, Bacon, and the March Hare, Marlowe—or Carroll, Bacon, and the Dormouse, Marlowe—or Alice was Shakespeare—or Bacon—or Carroll was the Mad Hatter. A pity Carroll is not alive today to settle it. Or Bacon. Or Marlowe. Or Shakespeare. The point is, if you're going to move, notify your post office. Unless you don't give a hoot about posterity.

If the Impressionists
Had Been Dentists

(A FANTASY EXPLORING THE
TRANSPOSITION OF TEMPERAMENT)

Dear Theo,

Will life never treat me decently? I am wracked by despair! My head is pounding! Mrs. Sol Schwimmer is suing me because I made her bridge as I felt it and not to fit her ridiculous mouth! That's right! I can't work to order like a common tradesman! I decided her bridge should be enormous and billowing, with wild, explosive teeth flaring up in every direction like fire! Now she is upset because it won't fit in her mouth! She is so bourgeois and stupid, I want to smash her! I tried forcing the false plate in but it sticks out like a star burst chandelier. Still, I find it beautiful. She claims she can't chew! What do I care whether she can chew or not! Theo, I can't go on like this much longer! I asked Cézanne if he would share an office with me, but he is old and infirm and unable to hold the instruments and they must be tied to his wrists but then he lacks accuracy and once inside a mouth, he knocks out more teeth than he saves. What to do?

Vincent

Dear Theo,

I took some dental X-rays this week that I thought were good. Degas saw them and was critical. He said the composition was bad. All the cavities were bunched in the lower left corner. I explained to him that's how Mrs. Slotkin's mouth looks, but he wouldn't listen! He said he hated the frames and mahogany was too heavy. When he left, I tore them to shreds! As if that was not enough, I attempted some root-canal work on Mrs. Wilma Zardis, but halfway through I became despondent. I realized suddenly that root-canal work is not what I want to do! I grew flushed and dizzy. I ran from the office into the air where I could breathe! I blacked out for several days and woke up at the seashore. When I returned, she was still in the chair. I completed her mouth out of obligation but I couldn't bring myself to sign it.

                                                                                      Vincent

Dear Theo,

Once again I am in need of funds. I know what a burden I must be to you, but who can I turn to? I need money for materials! I am working almost exclusively with dental floss now, improvising as I go along, and the results are exciting. God! I have not even a penny left for Novocaine! Today I pulled a tooth and had to anesthetize the patient by reading him some Dreiser. Help.

                                                                                      Vincent

Dear Theo,

Have decided to share offices with Gauguin. He is a fine dentist who specializes in bridgework, and he seems to like me. He was very complimentary about my work on Mr. Jay Greenglass. If you recall, I filled his lower seven, then despised the filling and tried to remove it. Greenglass was adamant and we went to court. There was a legal question of ownership, and on my lawyer's advice, I cleverly sued for the whole tooth and settled for the filling. Well, someone saw it lying in the corner of my office and he wants to put it in a show! They are already talking about a retrospective!

Vincent

Dear Theo,

I think it is a mistake to share offices with Gauguin. He is a disturbed man. He drinks Lavoris in large quantities. When I accused him, he flew into a rage and pulled my D.D.S. off the wall. In a calmer moment, I convinced him to try filling teeth outdoors and we worked in a meadow surrounded by greens and gold. He put caps on a Miss Angela Tonnato and I gave a temporary filling to Mr. Louis Kaufman. There we were, working together in the open air! Rows of blinding white teeth in the sunlight! Then a wind came up and blew Mr. Kaufman's toupee into the bushes. He darted for it and knocked Gauguin's instruments to the ground. Gauguin blamed me and tried to strike out but pushed Mr. Kaufman by mistake, causing him to sit down on the high-speed drill. Mr. Kaufman rocketed past me on a fly, taking Miss Tonnato with him. The upshot, Theo, is that Rifkin, Rifkin, Rifkin and Meltzer have attached my earnings. Send whatever you can.

Vincent

Dear Theo,

Toulouse-Lautrec is the saddest man in the world. He longs more than anything to be a great dentist, and he has real talent, but he's too short to reach his patients' mouths and too proud to stand on anything. Arms over his head, he gropes around their lips blindly, and yesterday, instead of putting caps on Mrs. Fitelson's teeth, he capped her chin. Meanwhile, my old friend Monet refuses to work on anything but very, very large mouths and Seurat, who is quite moody, has developed a method of cleaning one tooth at a time until he builds up what he calls "a full, fresh mouth." It has an architectural solidity to it, but is it dental work?

Vincent

Dear Theo,

I am in love. Claire Memling came in last week for an oral prophylaxis. (I had sent her a postcard telling her it had been six months since her last cleaning even though it had been only four days.) Theo, she drives me mad! Wild with desire! Her bite! I've never seen such a bite! Her teeth come together perfectly! Not like Mrs. Itkin's, whose lower teeth are forward of her uppers by an inch, giving her an underbite that resembles that of a werewolf! No! Claire's teeth close and meet! When this happens you know there is a God! And yet she's not too perfect. Not so flawless as to be uninteresting. She has a space between lower nine and eleven. Ten was lost during her adolescence. Suddenly and without warning it developed a cavity. It was removed rather easily (actually it fell out while she was talking) and was never replaced. "Nothing could replace lower ten," she told me. "It was more than a tooth, it had been my life to that point." The tooth was rarely discussed as she got older and I think she was only willing to speak of it to me because she trusts me. Oh, Theo, I love her. I was looking down into her mouth today and I was like a nervous young dental student again, dropping swabs and mirrors in there. Later I had my arms around her, showing her the proper way to brush. The sweet little fool was used to holding the brush still and moving her head from side to side. Next Thursday I will give her gas and ask her to marry me.

Vincent

Dear Theo,

Gauguin and I had another fight and he has left for Tahiti!
He was in the midst of an extraction when I disturbed him.
He had his knee on Mr. Nat Feldman's chest with the pliers
around the man's upper right molar. There was the usual
struggle and I had the misfortune to enter and ask Gauguin
if he had seen my felt hat. Distracted, Gauguin lost his grip
on the tooth and Feldman took advantage of the lapse to
bolt from the chair and race out of the office. Gauguin flew
into a frenzy! He held my head under the X-ray machine
for ten straight minutes and for several hours after I could
not blink my eyes in unison. Now I am lonely.

                                                    Vincent

Dear Theo,

All is lost! Today being the day I planned to ask Claire to
marry me, I was a bit tense. She was magnificent in her
white organdy dress, straw hat, and receding gums. As she
sat in the chair, the draining hook in her mouth, my heart
thundered. I tried to be romantic. I lowered the lights and
tried to move the conversation to gay topics. We both took a
little gas. When the moment seemed correct, I looked her
directly in the eye and said, "Please rinse." And she
laughed! Yes, Theo! She laughed at me and then grew
angry! "Do you think I could rinse for a man like you!?
What a joke!" I said, "Please, you don't understand." She
said, "I understand quite well! I could never rinse with
anyone but a licensed orthodontist! Why, the thought I
would rinse here! Get away from me!" And with that she
ran out weeping. Theo! I want to die! I see my face in the
mirror and I want to smash it! Smash it! Hope you are well.

                                                    Vincent

Dear Theo,

Yes, it's true. The ear on sale at Fleishman Brothers Novelty Shop is mine. I guess it was a foolish thing to do but I wanted to send Claire a birthday present last Sunday and every place was closed. Oh, well. Sometimes I wish I had listened to father and become a painter. It's not exciting but the life is regular.

Vincent

No Kaddish
for Weinstein

Weinstein lay under the covers, staring at the ceiling in a
depressed torpor. Outside, sheets of humid air rose from the
pavement in stifling waves. The sound of traffic was
deafening at this hour, and in addition to all this his bed
was on fire. Look at me, he thought. Fifty years old. Half a
century. Next year, I will be fifty-one. Then fifty-two. Using
this same reasoning, he could figure out his age as much as
five years in the future. So little time left, he thought, and so
much to accomplish. For one thing, he wanted to learn to
drive a car. Adelman, his friend who used to play dreidel
with him on Rush Street, had studied driving at the
Sorbonne. He could handle a car beautifully and had
already driven many places by himself. Weinstein had
made a few attempts to steer his father's Chevy but kept
winding up on the sidewalk.

He had been a precocious child. An intellectual. At
twelve, he had translated the poems of T. S. Eliot into
English, after some vandals had broken into the library and
translated them into French. And as if his high I.Q. did not
isolate him enough, he suffered untold injustices and
persecutions because of his religion, mostly from his parents.

True, the old man was a member of the synagogue, and his mother, too, but they could never accept the fact that their son was Jewish. "How did it happen?" his father asked, bewildered. My face looks Semitic, Weinstein thought every morning as he shaved. He had been mistaken several times for Robert Redford, but on each occasion it was by a blind person. Then there was Feinglass, his other boyhood friend: A Phi Beta Kappa. A labor spy, ratting on the workers. Then a convert to Marxism. A Communist agitator. Betrayed by the Party, he went to Hollywood and became the offscreen voice of a famous cartoon mouse. Ironic.

Weinstein had toyed with the Communists, too. To impress a girl at Rutgers, he had moved to Moscow and joined the Red Army. When he called her for a second date, she was pinned to someone else. Still, his rank of sergeant in the Russian infantry would hurt him later when he needed a security clearance in order to get the free appetizer with his dinner at Longchamps. Also, while at school he had organized some laboratory mice and led them in a strike over work conditions. Actually, it was not so much the politics as the poetry of Marxist theory that got him. He was positive that collectivization could work if everyone would learn the lyrics to "Rag Mop." "The withering away of the state" was a phrase that had stayed with him, ever since his uncle's nose had withered away in Saks Fifth Avenue one day. What, he wondered, can be learned about the true essence of social revolution? Only that it should never be attempted after eating Mexican food.

The Depression shattered Weinstein's Uncle Meyer, who kept his fortune under the mattress. When the market crashed, the government called in all mattresses, and Meyer became a pauper overnight. All that was left for him was to jump out the window, but he lacked the nerve and sat on a window sill of the Flatiron Building from 1930 to 1937.

"These kids with their pot and their sex," Uncle Meyer was fond of saying. "Do they know what it is to sit on a

window sill for seven years? There you see life! Of course,
everybody looks like ants. But each year Tessie—may she
rest in peace—made the Seder right out there on the ledge.
The family gathered round for Passover. Oy, nephew!
What's the world coming to when they have a bomb that
can kill more people than one look at Max Rifkin's
daughter?"

Weinstein's so-called friends had all knuckled under to
the House Un-American Activities Committee. Blotnick
was turned in by his own mother. Sharpstein was turned in
by his answering service. Weinstein had been called by the
committee and admitted he had given money to the
Russian War Relief, and then added, "Oh, yes, I bought
Stalin a dining-room set." He refused to name names but
said if the committee insisted he would give the heights of
the people he had met at meetings. In the end he panicked,
and instead of taking the Fifth Amendment, took the Third,
which enabled him to buy beer in Philadelphia on Sunday.

Weinstein finished shaving and got into the shower. He
lathered himself, while steaming water splashed down his
bulky back. He thought, Here I am at some fixed point in
time and space, taking a shower. I, Isaac Weinstein. One of
God's creatures. And then, stepping on the soap, he slid
across the floor and rammed his head into the towel rack. It
had been a bad week. The previous day, he had got a bad
haircut and was still not over the anxiety it caused him. At
first the barber had snipped judiciously, but soon Weinstein
realized he had gone too far. "Put some back!" he screamed
unreasonably.

"I can't," the barber said. "It won't stick."

"Well, then give it to me, Dominic! I want to take it with
me!"

"Once it's on the floor of the shop it's mine, Mr.
Weinstein."

"Like hell! I want my hair!"

He blustered and raged, and finally felt guilty and left. Goyim, he thought. One way or another, they get you.

Now he emerged from the hotel and walked up Eighth Avenue. Two men were mugging an elderly lady. My God, thought Weinstein, time was when one person could handle that job. Some city. Chaos everyplace. Kant was right: The mind imposes order. It also tells you how much to tip. What a wonderful thing, to be conscious! I wonder what the people in New Jersey do.

He was on his way to see Harriet about the alimony payments. He still loved Harriet, even though while they were married she had systematically attempted to commit adultery with all the *R*'s in the Manhattan telephone directory. He forgave her. But he should have suspected something when his best friend and Harriet took a house in Maine together for three years, without telling him where they were. He didn't *want* to see it—that was it. His sex life with Harriet had stopped early. He slept with her once on the night they first met, once on the evening of the first moon landing, and once to test if his back was all right after a slipped disc. "It's no damn good with you, Harriet," he used to complain. "You're too pure. Every time I have an urge for you I sublimate it by planting a tree in Israel. You remind me of my mother." (Molly Weinstein, may she rest in peace, who slaved for him and made the best stuffed derma in Chicago—a secret recipe until everyone realized she was putting in hashish.)

For lovemaking, Weinstein needed someone quite opposite. Like LuAnne, who made sex an art. The only trouble was she couldn't count to twenty without taking her shoes off. He once tried giving her a book on existentialism, but she ate it. Sexually, Weinstein had always felt inadequate. For one thing, he felt short. He was five-four in his stocking feet, although in someone else's stocking feet he could be as tall as five-six. Dr. Klein, his analyst, got him to see that jumping in front of a moving train was more hostile than self-destructive but in either case would ruin the crease in his pants. Klein was his third analyst. His first was a Jungian, who suggested they try a Ouija board. Before that, he attended "group," but when it came time for him to speak he got dizzy and could only recite the names of all the planets. His problem was women, and he knew it. He was impotent with any woman who finished college with higher than a B-minus average. He felt most at home with graduates of typing school, although if the woman did over sixty words a minute he panicked and could not perform.

Weinstein rang the bell to Harriet's apartment, and suddenly she was standing before him. Swelling to maculate giraffe, as usual, thought Weinstein. It was a private joke that neither of them understood.

"Hello, Harriet," he said.

"Oh, Ike," she said. "You needn't be so damn self-right-eous."

She was right. What a tactless thing to have said. He hated himself for it.

"How are the kids, Harriet?"

"We never had any kids, Ike."

"That's why I thought four hundred dollars a week was a lot for child support."

She bit her lip, Weinstein bit his lip. Then he bit her lip. "Harriet," he said, "I . . . I'm broke. Egg futures are down."

"I see. And can't you get help from your *shiksa?*"

"To you, any girl who's not Jewish is a *shiksa.*"

"Can we forget it?" Her voice was choked with recrimination. Weinstein had a sudden urge to kiss her, or if not her, somebody.

"Harriet, where did we go wrong?"

"We never faced reality."

"It wasn't my fault. You said it was north."

"Reality *is* north, Ike."

"No, Harriet. Empty dreams are north. Reality is west.
False hopes are east, and I think Louisiana is south."

She still had the power to arouse him. He reached out for
her, but she moved away and his hand came to rest in some
sour cream.

"Is that why you slept with your analyst?" he finally
blurted out. His face was knotted with rage. He felt like
fainting but couldn't remember the proper way to fall.

"That was therapy," she said coldly. "According to
Freud, sex is the royal road to the unconscious."

"Freud said *dreams* are the road to the unconscious."

"Sex, dreams—you're going to nit-pick?"

"Goodbye, Harriet."

It was no use. *Rien à dire, rien á faire.* Weinstein left and
walked over to Union Square. Suddenly hot tears burst
forth, as if from a broken dam. Hot, salty tears pent up for
ages rushed out in an unabashed wave of emotion. The
problem was, they were coming out of his ears. Look at this,
he thought; I can't even cry properly. He dabbed his ear
with Kleenex and went home.

Fine Times:
An Oral Memoir

The following are excerpts from the soon-to-be-published memoirs of Flo Guinness. Certainly the most colorful of all speakeasy owners during Prohibition, Big Flo, as her friends called her (many enemies called her that, too, mostly for convenience), emerges in these taped interviews as a woman with a lusty appetite for living, as well as a disappointed artist who had to give up her lifetime ambition to become a classical violinist, when she realized it would mean studying the violin. Here, for the first time, Big Flo speaks for herself.

Originally I danced at the Jewel Club in Chicago, for Ned Small. Ned was a shrewd businessman who made all his money by what we would now call "stealing." Of course, in those days it was quite different. Yes, sir, Ned had great charm—the kind you don't see today. He was famous for breaking both your legs if you disagreed with him. And he could do it, too, boys. He broke *more* legs! I'd say fifteen or sixteen legs a week was his average. But Ned was sweet on me, maybe 'cause I always told him straight to his face what I thought of him. "Ned," I told him over dinner once, "you're a mealymouth grifter with the morals of an alley cat." He laughed, but later that night I saw him looking up "mealymouth" in a dictionary. Anyhow, like I said, I danced at Ned Small's Jewel Club. I was his best dancer, boys—a dancer-*actress*. The other girls just hoofed, but I danced a little story. Like Venus emerging from her bath, only on Broadway and Forty-second Street, and she goes night-clubbing and dances till dawn and then has a massive coronary and loses control of the facial muscles on her left side. Sad stuff, boys. That's why I got respect.

One day, Ned Small calls me into his office and says, "Flo." (He always called me Flo, except when he got real mad at me. Then he'd call me Albert Schneiderman—I never knew why. Let's say the heart has strange ways.) So Ned says, "Flo, I want you to marry me." Well, you could've knocked me over with a feather. I started crying like a baby. "I mean it, Flo," he said. "I love you very deeply. It's not easy for me to say these things, but I want you to be the mother of my children. And if you don't I'll break both your legs." Two days later, to the minute, Ned Small and I tied the knot. Three days later, Ned was machine-gunned to death by the mob for spilling raisins on Al Capone's hat.

After that, of course, I was rich. First thing I did was buy my mother and father that farm they'd always talked about. They claimed they had never talked about a farm and actually wanted a car and some furs, but they gave it a try. Liked the rural life, too, although Dad got struck by lightning in the north forty and for six years afterward when asked his name could only say the word "Kleenex." As for me, three months later I was broke. Bad investments. I backed a whaling expedition in Cincinnati, on the advice of friends.

I danced for Big Ed Wheeler, who made bootleg hooch that was so strong it could only be sipped through a gas mask. Ed paid me three hundred dollars a week to do ten

shows, which in those days was big money. Hell, with tips I
made more than President Hoover. And he had to do
twelve shows. I went on at nine and eleven, and Hoover
went on at ten and two. Hoover was a good President, but
he was always sitting in his dressing room humming. It
drove me crazy. Then one day the owner of the Apex Club
saw my act and offered me five hundred dollars a week to
dance there. I put it squarely to Big Ed: "Ed, I got an offer
of five hundred bucks from Bill Hallorhan's Apex Club."

"Flo," he said, "if you can get five hundred a week, I
won't stand in your way." We shook hands and I went to
tell Bill Hallorhan the good news, but several of Big Ed's
friends had gotten there first and when I saw Bill Hallorhan
his physical condition had undergone a change and he was
now only a high-pitched voice that came from inside a cigar
box. He said he had decided to get out of show business,
leave Chicago, and settle somewhere closer to the equator. I
went on dancing for Big Ed Wheeler till the Capone mob
bought him out. I say, "bought him out," boys, but the
truth of it was Scarface Al offered him a tidy sum but
Wheeler said no. Later that day, he was having lunch at the
Rib and Chop House when his head burst into flames. No
one knew why.

I bought the Three Deuces with money I'd saved, and in
no time it was the hot spot in town. They all came—Babe
Ruth, Jack Dempsey, Jolson, Man o' War. Man o' War was
there every night. My God, how that horse could drink! I
remember once Babe Ruth had this crush on a showgirl
named Kelly Swain. He was so crazy about her he couldn't
keep his mind on baseball and twice greased his body,
thinking he was a famous channel swimmer. "Flo," he said
to me, "I'm nuts about this redhead, Kelly Swain. But she
hates sports. I lied and told her I give a course on
Wittgenstein, but I think she suspects something."

"Can you live without her, Babe?" I asked him.

"No, Flo. And it's affecting my concentration. Yesterday, I got four hits and stole two bases, but this is January and there are no games scheduled. I did it in my hotel room. Can you help me?"

I promised him I'd speak to Kelly, and the next day I stopped by the Golden Abattoir, where she was dancing. I said, "Kelly, the Bambino is nuts about you. He knows you like culture and he says if you date him he'll give up baseball and join the Martha Graham troupe."

Kelly looked me squarely in the eye and said, "Tell that palooka I didn't come all the way from Chippewa Falls to wind up with some overstuffed right fielder. I got big plans." Two years later, she married Lord Osgood Wellington Tuttle and became Lady Tuttle. Her husband gave up an ambassadorship to play shortstop for the Tigers. Jumpin' Joe Tuttle. He holds the record for most times beaned in the first inning.

Gambling? Boys, I was present when Nick the Greek got his name. There was a small-time gambler named Jake the Greek, and Nick called me and said, "Flo, I'd like to be The Greek." And I said, "I'm sorry, Nick, you're not Greek. And under New York State gambling laws it's forbidden." And he said, "I know, Flo, but my parents always wanted me to be called The Greek. You think you could arrange a lunch meeting with Jake?" I said, "Sure, but if he knows what it's for he won't show." And Nick said, "Try, Flo. It would mean a lot to me."

So the two met at the Grill Room of Monty's Steak House, which did not allow women but I could go there because Monty was a great friend of mine and didn't regard me as either male or female but, in his own words, "undefined protoplasm." We ordered the speciality of the house, ribs, which Monty had a way of preparing so they tasted like human fingers. Finally, Nick said, "Jake, I'd like to be called The Greek." And Jake turned pale and said,

"Look, Nick, if that's what you got me here for—" Well, boys, it got ugly. The two squared off. Then Nick said, "I'll tell you what I'll do. I'll cut you. High card gets to be called The Greek."

"But what if I win?" Jake said. "I'm *already* called The Greek."

"If you win, Jake, you can go through the phone book and pick any name you like. My compliments."

"No kidding?"

"Flo's the witness."

Well, you could feel the tension in that room. A deck of cards was brought out and they cut. Nick cut a queen, and Jake's hand was shaking. Then Jake cut an ace! Everybody let out a cheer, and Jake went through the phone book and selected the name Grover Lembeck. Everybody was happy, and from that day on women were allowed into Monty's, provided they could read hieroglyphics.

I remember once there was a big musical review at the Winter Garden, *Star-Spangled Vermin*. Jolson was the lead, but he quit because they wanted him to sing a song called "Kasha for Two," and he hated it. It had the line in it "Love is all, like a horse in a stall." Anyway, eventually it was sung by a young unknown named Felix Brompton, who was later arrested in a hotel room with a one-inch cardboard cutout of Helen Morgan. It was in all the papers. Well, Jolson come into the Three Deuces one night with Eddie Cantor, and he says to me, "Flo, I hear George Raft did his tap dance here last week." And I said, "No, Al. George has never been here." And he said, "If you let him do his tap dance, I'd like to sing." And I said, "Al, he was never here." And Al said, "Did he have any accompaniment on piano?" And I said, "Al, if you sing one note I'll personally throw you out." And with that Jolie got down on one knee and started on "Toot-Toot Tootsie." While he was singing, I sold the place, and by the time he was finished it was the Wing Ho Hand Laundry. Jolson never got over that or forgave me for it. On the way out, he tripped over a pile of shirts.

Slang Origins

How many of you have ever wondered where certain slang expressions come from? Like "She's the cat's pajamas," or to "take it on the lam." Neither have I. And yet for those who are interested in this sort of thing I have provided a brief guide to a few of the more interesting origins.

Unfortunately, time did not permit consulting any of the established works on the subject, and I was forced to either obtain the information from friends or fill in certain gaps by using my own common sense.

Take, for instance, the expression "to eat humble pie." During the reign of Louis the Fat, the culinary arts flourished in France to a degree unequaled anywhere. So obese was the French monarch that he had to be lowered onto the throne with a winch and packed into the seat itself with a large spatula. A typical dinner (according to DeRochet) consisted of a thin crêpe appetizer, some parsley, an ox, and custard. Food became the court obsession, and no other subject could be discussed under penalty of death. Members of a decadent aristocracy consumed incredible meals and even dressed as foods. DeRochet tells us that M. Monsant showed up at the coronation as a weiner, and Étienne Tisserant received papal dispensation to wed his favorite codfish. Desserts grew more and more elaborate and pies grew larger and larger until the minister of justice suffocated trying to eat a seven-foot "Jumbo Pie." *Jumbo* pie soon became *jumble* pie and "to eat a jumble pie" referred to any kind of humiliating act. When the Spanish seamen heard the word *jumble*, they pronounced it "humble," although many preferred to say nothing and simply grin.

Now, while "humble pie" goes back to the French, "take it on the lam" is English in origin. Years ago, in England, "lamming" was a game played with dice and a large tube of ointment. Each player in turn threw dice and then skipped around the room until he hemorrhaged. If a person threw seven or under he would say the word "quintz" and proceed to twirl in a frenzy. If he threw over seven, he was forced to give every player a portion of his feathers and was given a good "lamming." Three "lammings" and a player was "kwirled" or declared a moral bankrupt. Gradually any game with feathers was called "lamming" and feathers became "lams." To "take it on the lam" meant to put on feathers and later, to escape, although the transition is unclear.

Incidentally, if two of the players disagreed on the rules, we might say they "got into a beef." This term goes back to the Renaissance when a man would court a woman by stroking the side of her head with a slab of meat. If she pulled away, it meant she was spoken for. If, however, she assisted by clamping the meat to her face and pushing it all over her head, it meant she would marry him. The meat was kept by the bride's parents and worn as a hat on special occasions. If, however, the husband took another lover, the wife could dissolve the marriage by running with the meat to the town square and yelling, "With thine own beef, I do reject thee. Aroo! Aroo!" If a couple "took to the beef" or "had a beef" it meant they were quarreling.

Another marital custom gives us that eloquent and colorful expression of disdain, "to look down one's nose." In Persia it was considered a mark of great beauty for a woman to have a long nose. In fact, the longer the nose, the more desirable the female, up to a certain point. Then it became funny. When a man proposed to a beautiful woman he awaited her decision on bended knee as she "looked down her nose at him." If her nostrils twitched, he was accepted, but if she sharpened her nose with pumice and began pecking him on the neck and shoulders, it meant she loved another.

Now, we all know when someone is very dressed up, we say he looks "spiffy." The term owes its origin to Sir Oswald Spiffy, perhaps the most renowned fop of Victorian England. Heir to treacle millions, Spiffy squandered his money on clothes. It was said that at one time he owned enough handkerchiefs for all the men, women and children in Asia to blow their noses for seven years without stopping. Spiffy's sartorial innovations were legend, and he was the first man ever to wear gloves on his head. Because of extra-sensitive skin, Spiffy's underwear had to be made of the finest Nova Scotia salmon, carefully sliced by one particular tailor. His libertine attitudes involved him in several notorious scandals, and he eventually sued the government over the right to wear earmuffs while fondling a dwarf. In the end, Spiffy died a broken man in Chichester, his total wardrobe reduced to kneepads and a sombrero.

Looking "spiffy," then, is quite a compliment, and one who does is liable to be dressed "to beat the band," a turn-of-the-century expression that originated from the custom of attacking with clubs any symphony orchestra whose conductor smiled during Berlioz. "Beating the band" soon became a popular evening out, and people dressed up in their finest clothes, carrying with them sticks and rocks. The practice was finally abandoned during a performance of the *Symphonie fantastique* in New York when the entire string section suddenly stopped playing and exchanged gunfire with the first ten rows. Police ended the melee but not before a relative of J. P. Morgan's was wounded in the soft palate. After that, for a while at least, nobody dressed "to beat the band."

If you think some of the above derivations questionable, you might throw up your hands and say, "Fiddlesticks." This marvelous expression originated in Austria many years ago. Whenever a man in the banking profession announced his marriage to a circus pinhead, it was the custom for friends to present him with a bellows and a three-year supply of wax fruit. Legend has it that when Leo Rothschild made known his betrothal, a box of cello bows was delivered to him by mistake. When it was opened and found not to contain the traditional gift, he exclaimed, "What are these? Where are my bellows and fruit? Eh? All I rate is fiddlesticks!" The term "fiddlesticks" became a joke overnight in the taverns amongst the lower classes, who hated Leo Rothschild for never removing the comb from his hair after combing it. Eventually "fiddlesticks" meant any foolishness.

Well, I hope you've enjoyed some of these slang origins and that they stimulate you to investigate some on your own. And in case you were wondering about the term used to open this study, "the cat's pajamas," it goes back to an old burlesque routine of Chase and Rowe's, the two nutsy German professors. Dressed in oversized tails, Bill Rowe stole some poor victim's pajamas. Dave Chase, who got great mileage out of his "hard of hearing" specialty, would ask him:

CHASE: Ach, Herr Professor. Vot is dot bulge under your pocket?

ROWE: Dot? Dot's de chap's pajamas.

CHASE: The cat's pajamas? Ut mein Gott?

Audiences were convulsed by this sort of repartee and only a premature death of the team by strangulation kept them from stardom.

ABOUT THE AUTHOR
· · · · · · · · · · · · ·

After he was ejected from both New York University and City
College, WOODY ALLEN turned to a professional writing career, at
first for television and comedians. In 1964 he decided to become a
comedian himself.

In addition to his numerous nightclub and television appearances, Mr. Allen has made three comedy record albums of live
concert appearances and somehow found time to write two
long-running hits for Broadway, *Don't Drink the Water* and *Play It
Again, Sam* (the latter starring himself). His first film script,
written in 1964, was the enormously popular *What's New Pussycat?*
He has also written, directed and starred in five films to date:
*Take the Money and Run, Bananas, Everything You Always Wanted to
Know About Sex, Sleeper* and the soon to be released *Love and Death.*

Mr. Allen has written and appeared in his own television
specials and is a frequent contributor to *The New Yorker*, among
other periodicals.

His one regret in life is that he is not someone else.